Online Business Planning

How to Create a Better Business Plan Using
the Internet, Including a Complete,
Up-to-Date Resource Guide

By
Robert T. Gorman

CAREER PRESS
Franklin Lakes, NJ

ONLINE BUSINESS PLANNING
Cover design by Hub Graphics
Printed in the U.S.A. by Book-mart Press

To order this title, please call toll-free 1-800-CAREER-1 (NJ and Canada: 201-848-0310) to order using VISA or MasterCard, or for further information on books from Career Press.

The Career Press, Inc., 3 Tice Road, PO Box 687, Franklin Lakes, NJ 07417

Library of Congress Cataloging-in-Publication Data

Gorman, Robert T.
    Online business planning : how to create a better business plan
using the Internet, including a complete, up-to-date resource guide
/ by Robert T. Gorman.
        p.   cm.
    Includes index.
    ISBN 1-56414-369-4 (pbk.)
    1. Business planning.   2. Business planning--Computer network
resources--Directories.   3. Internet (Computer network)   I. Title.
HD30.28.G674   1998
025.06'6587012--dc21   98-30984

*To Ian and Ryan who sacrificed some quality family
time as I pursued this project.*

To Beth for being my biggest supporter and loyal proofreader.

To Mom for making me take typing in high school.

Thank you to Mike Snell for understanding the vision for this project, helping me to scrub the proposal, and getting it to Ron Fry at Career Press. Thank you also to Ron Fry for actually making this project a reality. Finally, special thanks to the hard-working staff at Career Press, including Betsy Sheldon, Ellen Scher, Mike Gaffney, and Sue Gruber.

Contents

Introduction

Welcome to *Online Business Planning*. You probably purchased this book because you have never created a business plan before and want to learn more before starting your business, or you are an experienced business planner and want to see how the Internet can help. Either way, you've come to the right source for information. *Online Business Planning* shows the beginner how to create a business plan and the professional how to create a better business plan using the Internet.

A business plan is nothing more than a communiqué explaining how you are going to make money from your idea or invention. Some plans may be stated verbally, such as, "Let's sell lemonade on Saturday," others may reach paper napkin status and become, "Let's sell lemonade on Saturday before the baseball game and charge 50¢ for a small glass and 75¢ for a large glass." However, neither of these plans covers the strategies and details that are required by potential investors, banks, venture capitalists, or your senior management.

Why do you need a business plan?

You don't. Anyone can start a business without a plan. In fact, many of the businesses being started today (even as you read this sentence) do not have a business plan. The owners and managers of these businesses have an idea or a "hunch" about what will make them successful, and they are simply acting on their instincts.

Consider the lemonade stand again. Would you ask your child, niece, or nephew to prepare a 20-page business plan to sell lemonade on the weekend? No, because the risk involved in setting up this business is far outweighed by the time and effort required to generate such a significant document. Still, you may have a few questions for the young entrepreneur, such as:

- On which day are you planning to sell lemonade?
- At what time?
- Where are you going to get the supplies?
- How much will they cost?

- How much are you going to charge?
- What will you do with the money you make?
- Who is going to help you?

Answers to these questions constitute the beginning of a business plan.

You need a business plan, not only because it may be a requirement of your bank, venture capitalist, or management, but also because it will help you to plan for the future. Your business plan shows you where you are today, where you want to be tomorrow, and how you are going to get there. For instance, your business plan:

- Causes you to evaluate your current situation, including your strengths, weaknesses, skills, personnel, and financial resources.
- Describes how you are going to meet the needs of your customers with your product and service benefits.
- Explains why your business is better than the competition, and how it will remain better in the future.
- Recognizes that things might go wrong in the future, and what alternatives you can pursue to correct the situation.

You create a business plan to help answer questions that are of interest to investors, bankers, or senior management, such as:

- What is the legal structure for your proposed business?
- What is the growth rate of your chosen industry?
- How will your product or service benefit customers?
- What did your market research reveal about the competition?
- How much profit will your business make this year? Next year?
- What type of organizational structure will you adopt?
- What will you do with the loan?

How can the Internet improve your business plan?

Traditionally, answers to many of the preceding questions were found in specialized libraries, back issues of magazines, and government archives. The research process was often long and tedious. Now, with the widespread availability of the Internet and World Wide Web, you have the opportunity to improve your plan by accessing current marketing, managerial, and financial information. All of this information can be obtained on personal computers at home or in the office.

Not only can you access statistical, financial, and economic data with the Internet, you can also find plenty of advice on:

- Business plan outlines.
- Market research.

- Target marketing.
- Choosing a franchise.
- Selecting a location.
- Advertising strategies.
- Obtaining bank loans.
- Raising venture capital.

All of this information is only a few mouseclicks away and can easily be incorporated into your business plan.

Organization of the book

Online Business Planning is divided into two parts: Creating a Business Plan and Creating a Better Business Plan Using the Internet. The first part is designed to help individuals with little or no business planning experience create a business plan. It covers the basic elements that must be included in a business plan. The second part is designed to help individuals who are familiar with business plans access some of the powerful data that is available through the Internet. However, it will only be a matter of time before some novices are surfing the Web, while other more experienced planners are brushing up on the business concepts.

Part I: Creating a business plan

Although the format and content of all business plans vary widely from company to company, all plans must address a common set of topics that are of interest to investors, bankers, and managers. The first part of *Online Business Planning* takes you through a common set of topics, which includes creating a description of your business, developing a marketing strategy, putting together a management team, and generating a set of financial projections. In addition, the first part of the book includes a sample business plan for a clothing manufacturer called South Mill.

Part II: Creating a better business plan using the Internet

Through the Internet, business planners are now able to access a wide variety of information that was previously only available through back issues of magazines, government archives, and public libraries. *Online Business Planning* shows you where this information can be found and how you can incorporate it into your business plan. For instance, the book walks you through Internet sites that cover business plan outlines, industry growth opportunities, market research ideas, raising venture capital, and many more.

Where to begin

If you are a beginner and not familiar with the structure and content of business plans, read the first chapter of this book and then surf through some of the Internet sites that provide business plan outlines. In addition to out-lines, many of these sites also have a wealth of information on business planning strategies and how you can incorporate them into your plan. This should give you an excellent overview of all of the topics you will need to cover in your business plan.

If you are an experienced planner, then it's up to you to select a starting point. Simply turn to the second part of the book and select a chapter. Each Internet chapter provides detailed instructions on how to access some of the most informative business planning sites on the World Wide Web, as well as a brief narrative on many other sites.

Part I

Creating a Business Plan

Chapter 1

Overview of Your Business Plan

Key points:

♦ The first three or four pages of your business plan must capture the reader's attention.

♦ Your business plan should include a cover sheet, executive summary, statement of purpose, and table of contents.

♦ The executive summary captures the key elements of the plan, including business description, marketing strategy, management team, and financial performance.

Before you start blasting away with your word processing and spreadsheet software, consider why you are creating a business plan. Do you need startup money? A bank loan for new equipment or inventory? Financing for expansion? Or a "yardstick" to measure your performance against stated goals and objectives? Although most business plans cover certain "core" material, the purpose for developing your plan will determine in part some of its format and content.

According to the U.S. Small Business Administration (SBA), your business plan should cover the following four distinct sections:

1. The description of the business.
2. The marketing plan.
3. The financial management plan.
4. The management plan.

Additionally, your business plan should include an executive summary, supporting documents, and financial projections.

Don't be misled by the "small" in SBA, because these guidelines generally work very well for businesses of any size. In fact, these guidelines were probably developed by very large businesses and passed down to smaller businesses as "the correct approach."

Questions to be answered in your business plan

The following is a list of questions that you should answer in your business plan. These are the questions that bankers, investors, or your management will want answered. You may need to modify this list to ensure that you are only covering those items that are important for your business.

Description of the business:

♦ What business are you in?

♦ What is the name of your business? When did you start it?

♦ Is it a proprietorship, partnership, or corporation?

♦ Are you a manufacturer, merchandiser, or service business?

♦ What products and services are you selling?

♦ Is it a franchise business, a startup, an expansion, or an acquisition?

♦ How fast is it going to grow in sales and profitability?

♦ What is your mission? What are your corresponding goals and objectives?

Products and services:

♦ What benefits do your products and services offer customers?

♦ How are your products and services better than competing alternatives?

♦ What is your best-selling product?

♦ Are you expanding product lines? Or creating a whole new product line?

Industry and market analysis:

♦ What is the structure of the industry?

♦ How large is your industry? How fast is it growing?

♦ What impact does technology have on the industry?

♦ What are the barriers to entering and exiting the industry?

♦ How large are the markets? How fast are they growing?

♦ What market trends are affecting the industry?

Customers:

♦ How many potential customers are in your target market?

♦ What is your share of this market?

♦ What do they buy from your business? How much do they buy?

♦ What key variables can you use to separate them into groups?

♦ How are you going to retain existing customers?

Market research:
- ♦ What competitors do your prospects consider when evaluating alternatives?
- ♦ Do your prospective customers have a contract with a competitor?
- ♦ What are your customer preferences for color, styling, service levels, and payment?
- ♦ Why did your prospects choose a competitor?
- ♦ How much do your competitors charge for their products and services?

Competition:
- ♦ Who are your direct and indirect competitors?
- ♦ How large are your competitors? In sales? In profits?
- ♦ What are your competitor segments?
- ♦ How is your business better than theirs?
- ♦ What are the weaknesses of your direct competitors?

Marketing strategy:
- ♦ What are your product and service benefits?
- ♦ How are you pricing your products and services?
- ♦ What are your channels of distribution?
- ♦ Where is your business located?
- ♦ How large is your marketing budget?

Management:
- ♦ Why are you and your management team going to be successful?
- ♦ What previous experience do you have in this business?
- ♦ Are you lacking any managerial skills? How will you get these skills?
- ♦ What type of organizational structure does your business have?
- ♦ What are the responsibilities of each member of the management team?

Personnel:
- ♦ How many people work for your business?
- ♦ Are you going to hire more?
- ♦ How do you recruit and train employees?

Finances:
- ♦ Is you business profitable? If not, when will it be profitable?
- ♦ How fast will your sales and profits grow in the next three years?

- What is your business worth?
- Does your business have positive or negative cash flow?
- What is your breakeven point?

Note that the preceding questions could have included sections on manufacturing, operations, and research and development. If these factors will determine your success, then be sure to include them in your business plan. For instance, the business plan for South Mill, Inc., referred to throughout this book, contains an entire section on manufacturing, because this company believes that its flexible production capability gives it a competitive advantage in the marketplace.

How long should your business plan be?

The length of your business plan is strictly dependent on what you want to accomplish, how thoroughly you analyze your markets, and the number of financial projections you include. As stated previously, business plans range from verbal statements to paper napkin drawings to documents that are in excess of 50 pages. From the following section you might estimate that your plan will require a single page for every one of the business plan elements recommended by the SBA.

Elements of a business plan

The following elements of a business plan are published on the SBA Web site, and provide a good starting place for your business plan outline. Source: U.S. Small Business Administration
URL: http://www.sbaonline.sba.gov/starting/businessplan.html

1. Cover sheet
2. Statement of purpose
3. Table of contents
   I.   The business

      A.   Description of business
      B.   Marketing
      C.   Competition
      D.   Operating procedures
      E.   Personnel
      F.   Business insurance
      G.   Financial data

   II.   Financial data

      A.   Loan applications
      B.   Capital equipment and supply list
      C.   Balance sheet
      D.   Breakeven analysis
      E.   Pro forma income projections (profit & loss statements)

           1.   Three-year summary
           2.   Detail by month, first year
           3.   Detail by quarters, second and third years
           4.   Assumptions upon which projections were based
    F.   Pro-forma cash flow
  III.   Supporting documents
      A.   Tax returns of principals for last three years
      B.   Personal financial statement (all banks have these forms)
      C.   For franchises, a copy of franchise contract and all supporting documents provided by the franchiser
      D.   Copy of proposed lease or purchase agreement for building space
      E.   Copy of licenses and other legal documents
      F.   Copy of resumes of all principals
      G.   Copies of letters of intent from suppliers, etc.

The first three or four pages of your business plan

Imagine that you have less than 10 minutes to interest your boss, a potential investor, or someone you want to hire in your business plan. What key aspects of your business will you describe to keep them from moving on to their next opportunity? After all, these are busy people who may be presented with multiple business plans and new business opportunities every day.

Much like a television commercial or magazine advertisement, the first three or four pages of your business plan are written to gain attention and to get the readers to ask for more information. After you get them hooked, then you can negotiate the terms of a loan, a potential investment, or whether they might be interested in working for your company. The first pages of your business plan include the following:

- ◆ Cover sheet
- ◆ Executive summary
- ◆ Statement of purpose
- ◆ Table of contents

Although you cannot prepare these pages until you have finished the rest of your business plan, look at them now, and note some of the key points that you should be able to extract from the entire document.

Cover sheet

The purpose of the cover sheet is not only to introduce your company name, but also to present a professional appearance and to make it as easy as possible for someone to find you if they have additional questions. Keep in mind that once you submit your plan to bankers, prospective investors, or venture capitalists, it may be passed around to a variety of individuals, such as lawyers and accountants, for a second opinion.

BUSINESS PLAN

South Mill, Inc.
1234 West Main Street
Anywhere, Georgia 43112
(303) 555-1818

October 20, 1998

Contact:
Howard T. McBain
President

Copy ___ of ____

Proprietary & Confidential
Not for reproduction

For financing proposals, you should typically include your name or a contact person, the appropriate title for the contact, the name of the business, its address, a phone number, and the publication date. Other items you may want to consider are:

- ◆ Fax number.
- ◆ E-mail ID.
- ◆ Company logo.
- ◆ Standard Industrial Classification (SIC) code.

◆ The number of copies of the plan that have been distributed, for example, copy 3 of 5.

◆ A statement of confidentiality if you don't want your plan "passed around."

For a business plan that is to be used for internal purposes only and not shared with anyone outside your company, your name, the name of the project, and the date should be sufficient information.

Executive summary

The executive summary contains one or two of the most important pages in your business plan. You do not simply introduce your company to prospective investors, bankers, or senior management on these pages—you sell them your idea. Your executive summary must at least stimulate enough interest so that readers will turn to the table of contents for more information.

Remember that you do not have much time to capture someone's attention, because they may devote only a few minutes to reading your executive summary. It must clearly state what you are trying to accomplish in as few words as possible. Each paragraph must capture the key elements of your marketing, management, and financing strategy.

A sample executive summary

South Mill is a vertically integrated manufacturer of high-quality polo shirts and T-shirts for men and women. The company plans to increase sales and profitability in the next three years by selling high-value products to wholesalers and retailers. The company expects to continue its sales growth of nearly 45 percent per year, to $13.6 million by the year 2000, while maintaining net profits at 8.5 percent of sales.

South Mill will meet its growth objectives by continuing to cost-effectively manufacture higher-quality polo shirts and T-shirts and selling them to a wider variety of customers than other competitors in the industry. South Mill's continued expansion builds on its strategy to invest in the latest technology and utilization of flexible manufacturing methods.

South Mill will continue to be an innovator in the apparel industry by introducing additional polo shirts and T-shirt improvements, such as fiber-reactive dyes to reduce fading, and rib-knit collars that last longer. The company will also continue to manufacture products with unique styling for its retail and wholesale customers, by capitalizing on its "made-to-order" flexible production capabilities.

Look at the executive summary for South Mill, Inc., and note some of the key items that are mentioned in the first paragraph. The first sentence tells what type of business it is (vertically integrated manufacturer) and what it produces (high-quality polo shirts and T-shirts). The second sentence describes South Mill's marketing plan by addressing its pricing strategy (high-value products) and its target market (retailers and wholesalers). The third sentence explicitly states its growth objectives in terms of sales ($13.6 million in the year 2000) and its profits (8.5 percent of sales).

As you write your executive summary, keep in mind that it must be clear and concise and touch on all of the business plan elements. It's not necessary to cover every detail in your first four sentences, but by the end of one, and not more than two pages, readers must be told what you are trying to do in a language they can understand.

Statement of purpose

For financing proposals, where you are seeking money from banks or investors, include a statement of purpose in your executive summary. The statement of purpose identifies the who, how much, and why of your business plan by answering the following questions:

- How much money is required?
- What will you use the money for—equipment, building, working capital?
- How will the funding lead to increased sales and/or profits?
- When and how will the money be repaid?

A sample statement of purpose

In order to continue its expansion, South Mill seeks a total loan of $500,000 to increase its current manufacturing capacity at its plant in Anywhere, Georgia. The breakdown of this amount is as follows: $300,000 would be used to increase the size of its existing plant, including adding 7,000 square feet of floor space and upgrading electrical power for the entire building; $120,000 to purchase new knitting and dyeing machinery; and $80,000 to improve its working capital position. The expansion will help South Mill to reduce its current backlog of orders, increase total sales, and improve profitability.

If you are seeking a loan from a bank, as South Mill is, make sure that the pro forma financial statements contained in your business plan support repayment of the loan. For instance, South Mill's expansion over the next three years will provide higher profits and give it the ability to make interest and principal payments on the proposed loan.

Table of contents

Depending on the length of your executive summary, the table of contents will be the third or fourth page of your business plan. It follows your cover page, executive summary, and statement of purpose, and should be broken into at least three parts: the business, financial data, and appendices. Depending on the length and complexity of your plan, the business part could be divided again into three parts: business description, marketing, and management. However, the financial data should always be separated into its own part because many investors may turn there after reading your executive summary.

A sample table of contents

Chapter 2

Description of Your Business

Questions to be answered in this chapter:
- What business are you in?
- What is the name of your business? When did you start it?
- Is it a proprietorship, partnership, or corporation?
- Are you a manufacturer, merchandiser, or service business?
- What products and services are you selling?
- Is it a franchise business, a startup, an expansion, or an acquisition?
- How fast is it going to grow in sales and profitability?
- What is your mission? What are your corresponding goals and objectives?

The "description of business" section of your business plan summarizes for readers what your business has done in the past, what it is going to do in the future, and how it is going to get there. Think of this section as providing a little more information than your executive summary, but not all of the supporting details contained in the rest of your plan. The most important question that you must answer in this section of your business plan is "what business are you in?"

If you answer the question too narrowly, you may miss out on larger opportunities. If you answer the question too broadly, you will never be able to focus on the business at hand. For example, imagine that you owned a movie theater and someone asked you, "What business are you in?" You might provide the narrow response and say "I am in the movie theater business," or you might provide the broad response and say, "I am in the entertainment business." Either of these responses is acceptable depending on what your mission and objectives are.

How you think of your business will have a bearing on many of the decisions that you will have to make in the future. Much like the captain of a ship, you must establish objectives to get from point A to point B. For example, if you want to become a $50-million company in five years, then you will have to be a $5-million company next year. Along the way, distractions will develop, such as raw material shortages, alternative technologies, or new competition, and cause your business to travel off course. However, if you have established clear and concise objectives, then you will always know where you are relative to your destination and be able correct the situation by charting a new course.

Once you have established what business you are in, identifying your target markets, customers, and competitors will become much easier. For this section of your business plan you will also want to highlight the key elements of your business, including your financial performance, product benefits, marketing strategy, and management capabilities.

What business are you in?

Answering this famous question (posed by Harvard's Theodore Levitt), might open a whole new world of opportunity for your business and take it to undreamed-of levels of success. Answering it incorrectly might cause your business to stagnate or even fail.

Following are two separate answers to the question, "What business are you in?" The first is from Clearview Cinema Group, Inc., and the second is from The Walt Disney Company. Both were taken from documents that were filed with the Securities and Exchange Commission (SEC) through their EDGAR OnLine service.

What business is the Clearview Cinema Group, Inc., in?	What business is The Walt Disney Company in?
Clearview Cinema Group, Inc., is a regional motion picture exhibitor that operates in-town multiplex theaters primarily located in affluent suburban communities in the New York/New Jersey metropolitan area.	The Walt Disney Company is a diversified international entertainment company with operations in the businesses of Creative Content, Broadcasting, and Theme Parks and Resorts.

Although it can be argued that both Clearview and Disney provide entertainment for consumers, look at the differences between how they answered the question, "What business are you in?" Clearview took the narrow view and decided that it is only in the regional motion picture exhibition business, while Disney approached the subject broadly and decided that it is in the entertainment business.

Clearview's answer to this question has a bearing on how it will operate over the coming years. Its growth in sales and profits will be derived from either increasing viewership at its existing movie theaters or its acquisition of new movie theaters. It would not appear that Clearview is planning to grow by diversifying into other areas of the entertainment industry, such as video rental stores or theme parks.

Disney, on the other hand, is a diversified international entertainment company with many lines of business. Its future growth could also come from expanding its existing lines of business, or because it is an entertainment company, it could also branch out into new lines of business. Perhaps even movie theaters.

How Clearview and Disney answered the question "What business are you in?" has laid the groundwork for any potential growth opportunities these two companies might pursue in the future.

Did either of these companies answer the question incorrectly? It's impossible to say. However, by looking at their respective industries, markets, customers, and competitors, these companies have decided that their greatest opportunities for success lie within these businesses. Because Clearview is a much smaller business than Disney, it believes that it can achieve its growth objectives by concentrating solely on the movie theater business. Disney, on the other hand, is a much larger business that has to diversify in order to meet its growth objectives. After all, how many theme parks can it open or movies can it produce to keep its profits growing at 30 percent annually?

A rule of thumb would be that the smaller your business, the more focused it should be on a single line of business. If Clearview had said that it was in the entertainment business and wanted to undertake all of Disney's businesses, then investors would become very skeptical and believe that the company was spreading its resources too thinly.

Additional considerations for your business description

Once you have decided what business you are in, then you must provide readers of your plan with a complete description of the business. Information that they will be most interested to learn include your financial performance, product benefits, marketing strategy, and management capabilities.

The following is the description of business for South Mill, Inc. Take a moment to study it, and look at some of the key items that are presented in this section of its business plan.

Sample description of business

South Mill is a vertically integrated manufacturer of high-quality polo shirts and T-shirts for men and women. The company plans to increase sales and profitability by selling high-value products to a wide variety of customers. South Mill sells its clothing to companies such as Ralph Lauren, Brooks Brothers, and Neiman Marcus. Additionally, the company sells its clothing, using its own brand name, to wholesale and retail customers such as Kmart and Sears. The company has increased net sales from $1.5 million in 1994 to $4.5 million in 1997, a compound annual growth rate of nearly 45 percent, and has been profitable since 1990.

South Mill was incorporated in November 1987 by certain members of the management team who collectively have more than 50 years of industry experience. Their vision was to cost-effectively manufacture higher-quality polo shirts and T-shirts and sell to a wider variety of customers than other competitors in the industry. To meet the objective of producing low-cost, high-quality clothing, South Mill invested in the latest technology available to manufacturers.

Since the business started, South Mill has been a leading manufacturer of polo shirts and T-shirts and has set new standards for styling and quality. The company was first to market with competitively priced clothing that used fiber-reactive dyes to reduce fading and rib-knit collars with more thickness to resist curling. Market acceptance of these products was rapid, and the company has been able to expand its sales and profitability every year by reaching more customer segments. In 1991, South Mill started manufacturing its line of polo shirts and T-shirts with long sleeves to diversify its product mix and use its production capacity more efficiently.

Additionally, South Mill works with customers to develop new products with unique styling. This gives the company a competitive advantage, because most of its competitors lack the flexible manufacturing facilities necessary to offer "made-to-order" services to their customers. That often leads the company to be chosen as the "manufacturer of choice" by large retailers and wholesalers.

The first sentence tells readers what business South Mill is in: "South Mill is a vertically integrated manufacturer of high-quality polo shirts and T-shirts for men and women." Note that South Mill has taken the narrow approach in deciding what business it is in. Although a broader approach, such as "South Mill is a vertically integrated manufacturer of clothing for men and women," might give it more opportunity to develop other articles of clothing for different markets, it has decided to focus strictly on polo shirts and T-shirts for men and women.

The next sentence addresses the key element of South Mill's marketing strategy by stating that it plans to sell "high-value products to a wide variety of customers." Although most investors will applaud the concept of selling "high-value" products because they are usually associated with price premiums, some may get nervous at the thought of trying to meet the needs of "a wide variety of customers." It is often difficult for a business to meet the needs of a *few* customers, let alone a wide variety of customers. However, South Mill then follows up by explaining that it has been able to do this successfully in the past by citing examples of some of its customers.

The fifth sentence says what every investor, banker, or manager wants to hear: "The company has increased net sales from $1.5 million in 1994 to $4.5 million in 1997, a compound annual growth rate of nearly 45 percent, and has been profitable since 1990." Any company that has been able to grow its sales every year for the past four years, achieve an annual growth rate of 45 percent, and still remain profitable is worth a second look.

The remaining three paragraphs of South Mill's description of business provide insights into its management team that "collectively have more than

50 years of industry experience," its competitive advantage of being a low-cost producer, and its product benefits that have "set new standards for styling and quality." Finally, South Mill points out that it has become the "manufacturer of choice" by some of the largest customers in the market.

There are many ways for you to describe your business to potential investors, bankers, or managers, but the basic outline will always be the same. Start by answering the question, "What business am I in?" and follow it with key points about your marketing strategy, financial performance, and management experience.

Why is it so important to figure out what business you are really in? It's important because you need to recognize that some companies that are not your direct competitors today may be tomorrow. A classic example can be found in the railroad industry. Early on, these companies did not recognize that they were in the transportation business (they thought they were in the railroad business) and soon began losing customers to automobile manufacturers and commercial airlines.

Business form

The "description of business" section must also mention the business form or legal structure that you have selected for the business. The four types of legal structures are sole proprietorships, partnerships, corporations, and limited liability companies. Your selection should take into consideration the goals of the business and the tax and personal liability consequences that are unique to each legal structure.

If you are starting a home-based business to sell newsletter subscriptions, it is more than likely that you will select the sole proprietorship as the legal structure for your business. It is easy to set up, does not require any legal form of business organization, and requires the least amount of tax reporting to state and federal agencies.

On the other hand, if you are planning to purchase a factory to build jet airplanes, you will certainly consider incorporating your business. Although a corporation is much more difficult to set up than a proprietorship and it requires expert legal advice and significant resources to prepare tax returns, it provides limited liability for the owners in the event of a lawsuit.

Before finalizing your decision, you should consult an attorney and be aware of the documents that must be filed with federal, state, and local governments.

Mission and vision statements

Many businesses create mission and vision statements as part of their business plan. Through these statements, companies endeavor to create an overriding purpose for their business. They attempt to go beyond the "What business are you in?" question by crafting a few sentences that will define the company's direction in the future.

Have you ever asked anyone what they were doing and received an answer that described the end result of their current actions? For instance, if you asked a gardener who was digging holes with a shovel what she was do-ing, she might reply, "I am planting flowers." Or if you asked a homeowner who was painting the bedroom walls what he was doing, he might answer, "I am decorating the room."

Why didn't the gardener say, "I am digging holes," or the homeowner say, "I am painting the walls." Instead of telling you the obvious, these individuals described to you the final outcome of their current actions—or their mission. Similarly, as you describe your business, don't tell people what your current actions are, tell them what the final outcome will be.

In order for your company to be successful, you must understand what business you are in. Start with the end result, and work backwards. Define your mission statement, then create the goals and objectives that will help you to accomplish your mission. For instance, if your mission is to plant flow-ers, then you must dig holes first. If your vision is a beautiful landscape, then you must dig holes and then plant flowers.

Once you have a mission, with corresponding goals and objectives, read-ers of your business plan will want to know how you will be successful in your chosen industry. They will want to know whether you are trying to dig holes in concrete or moist topsoil.

Following are mission and vision statements from some of the premiere companies in the world. These were obtained from the online annual reports of the respective companies.

Coca-Cola

http://www.cocacola.com/co/mission.html

We exist to create value for our share owners on a long-term basis by building a business that enhances The Coca-Cola Company's trademarks. This also is our ultimate commitment....As the world's largest beverage com-pany, we refresh the world. We do this by developing superior soft drinks, both carbonated and noncarbonated, and profitable nonalcoholic beverage systems that create value for our Company, our bottling partners, and our customers.

Ford Motor Company

http://www.ford.com/corporate-info/stockholder/anreport/growth.html

Ford's vision is to be the leading automotive company in the world. That doesn't mean the biggest; it means the best. For us, leadership means prod-uct excellence, while at the same time being the best in customer satisfaction, value, cost, quality, and profitability.

McDonald's

http://www.mcdonalds.com/corporate/investor/index.html

McDonald's vision is to dominate the global food service industry. Global dominance means setting the performance standard for customer satisfaction and increasing market share and profitability through successfully implementing our Convenience, Value, and Execution Strategies.

Microsoft

http://www.microsoft.com/mscorp/

Since its inception in 1975, Microsoft's mission has been to create software for the personal computer that empowers and enriches people in the workplace, at school, and at home. Microsoft's early vision of a computer on every desk and in every home is coupled today with a strong commitment to Internet-related technologies that expand the power and reach of the PC and its users. As the world's leading software provider, Microsoft strives to produce innovative products that meet customers' evolving needs.

In summary, some of the key ideas from the mission and vision statements are as follows:

♦ Coca-Cola wants to "refresh the world."
♦ Ford is going to be "the leading automotive company in the world."
♦ McDonald's wants to "dominate the global food service industry."
♦ Microsoft creates "software for the personal computer that empowers and enriches people in the workplace, at school, and at home."

Goals and objectives

Goals and objectives tell your audience how you will accomplish your mission. Goals tend to be general statements, such as "dominating the market" and "increasing profitability," while objectives are quantifiable actions that are related to specific goals. For instance, from the South Mill example, one of the company's goals is to increase sales, with a specific objective of reaching $13.6 million by the year 2000.

Suppose your mission is to become the largest retailer in your home state. Because it is unlikely that you will succeed overnight (unless your business has a name like Sears or Kmart), you will probably need a series of intermediary steps to accomplish this mission. You might start by setting a goal of selling more apparel in the coming year with an objective of running quarterly sales in men's and women's clothing.

The following are goals and objectives for the same companies whose mission statements were reviewed previously.

Coca-Cola

http://www.cocacola.com/co/chairman97.html

Looking ahead over the long term, we see no reason to change our ambitious and long-held targets; we still expect worldwide volume growth of 7 to 8 percent per year....We intend to keep on working to make our brands always special, different, and better in the minds and hearts of our consumers and customers. We will serve more customers with more promotions and more strategies to drive their businesses and ours, and we will take more steps to strengthen and align the bottling system that serves them.

Ford Motor Company

http://www.ford.com/finaninvest/stockholder/stock97/index.htm

We've publicly stated financial goals for our automotive business once again in 1998....For our automotive business, we're targeting a 5-percent return on sales in North America, profitability in Europe, and a breakeven position in South America. A reduction in total costs from 1997 of $1 billion, at constant volume and mix. And a reduction in capital spending.

McDonald's

http://www.mcdonalds.com/corporate/investor/reports/annualreport/index.html

Our first priority is to improve restaurant operations. To create a meaningful gap between McDonald's and the competition, we must excel. We must be the best. We'll make hotter, fresher food that's better tasting. We'll serve customers faster, make sure they get what they ordered, and be friendlier while doing it.

Microsoft

http://www.microsoft.com/msft/ar97/bill_letter/bill_letter.htm

Our top priority in fiscal 1998 is simplicity: reducing the total cost of ownership and reducing complexity. We will need to keep this focus even as we roll out numerous products, and while competitors are battling with us on many fronts.

In summary, the "Description of Business" section of your business plan lets readers know who you are, what you do, and where you want to go. In this section, you must answer the question, "What business are you in?" If you are going to make golf clubs for a living, don't write a plan that says you are in the outdoor recreation business (this is way too broad for a golf club manufacturer). As part of this section you should also consider adding a mission or vision statement that is supported by concrete goals and objectives.

Chapter 3

Products and Services

Questions to be answered in this chapter:

♦ What benefits do your products and services offer customers?

♦ How are your products and services better than your competitors'?

♦ What is your best-selling product?

♦ Are you expanding product lines? Or creating a whole new line?

Product and service benefits

Light beer is less filling. Flame broiling tastes better. Skin cream can make you look younger. The manufacturers and retailers of these products—beer, burgers, skin cream—are trying to sell you the benefits of their products, not their features. The brewery may describe light beer as having 30 percent fewer calories than regular beer, but what you will hear and see in the television commercial is that it is less filling.

As you begin writing product and service descriptions for your business plan, consider the benefits being offered to potential consumers. Don't concentrate on product descriptions and features. Explain how your product benefits the customer. A feature simply describes the product, while a benefit focuses on the needs of customers. A benefit can satisfy a prospect's needs in a variety of ways, such as being the most economical, the fastest, or the most entertaining.

In the following table you will notice that the benefits appeal to the prospects' needs with a description of how those needs will be satisfied.

Product	Feature	Benefit
Phone service	One-second timing	More economical because calls are not rounded to nearest minute
Hamburgers	Flame broiled	Tastes better
Superstore	More products	Wider selection offers one-stop shopping
Light beer	30 percent fewer calories	Less filling
Golf club	Titanium shaft	Hit the ball further
Satellite television	200 channels	Better variety of programming than cable television
Automobile	3.8 V8 engine	Quicker acceleration

Financial performance

In addition to describing product and service benefits, your business plan should help readers see the past or anticipated financial performance for individual products and services. For instance, look at the following sample product description for Super PC. Its product lines have been broken down into two categories: personal computers and peripherals. Then the sales revenue and average selling price for these product categories have been itemized for two consecutive years. Not only has Super PC been able to grow its product lines year-over-year, but it also has been able to increase the average selling price of its computers and peripherals during the same period.

Sample product description

Super PC's high-quality personal computers and peripherals meet consumer preferences for more speed and larger memory capacity. The company's computer products include a variety of processors and memory configurations. Processing speeds of 233Mhz, 266Mhz, 300Mhz, and 400Mhz can be matched with memory modules ranging from 32MB to 512MB. Super PC also distributes the latest printing and monitor technology to complement its line of personal computers.

The company believes that certain design and assembly features enhance the quality and appeal of its computers relative to most competitors:

♦ Super PCs computers are faster and have more memory capacity.

♦ Super PC provides numerous internal "slots" that offer consumers the flexibility to add peripherals.

♦ Super PC uses gold-plated connectors between all of its peripherals to ensure the highest reliability.

♦ All of Super PC's components meet the most rigorous military specifications for durability and longevity.

♦ Super PC uses the latest software available to ensure that components reach optimum performance.

♦ Super PC offers extended warranties for added consumer protection against failure.

The sales mix for personal computers and peripherals for the years ended December 31, 1996 and 1997, in sales and the average sales price per unit are as follows:

Years ended December 31	1997 Sales	1997 Units	1997 Avg	1996 Sales	1996 Units	1996 Avg
Computers	$68,312	40	$1,708	$58,333	38	$1,535
Peripherals	$38,302	109	$351	$32,131	95	$338
Total/Avg.	$106,614	149	$715	$90,464	133	$680

Historically, Super PC's sales have been derived predominantly from personal computers. However, since introducing peripheral products in 1992, the company has increased peripheral sales in order to diversify its product mix and increase the average sales per customer.

If you are having trouble figuring out the benefits that your product or service will offer customers, it is time to rethink your business. You must be able to point to one or two things that differentiate your product or service from competing alternatives and describe how they will benefit consumers. See Chapter 6 on Market Research for some helpful ideas on identifying product and service benefits.

Chapter 4

Industry and Market Analysis

Questions to be answered in this section:

- What is the structure of the industry?
- How large is your industry? How fast is it growing?
- What impact does technology have on the industry?
- What are the barriers to entering and exiting the industry?
- How large are the markets? How fast are they growing?
- What market trends are affecting the industry?

An industry and market analysis will uncover opportunities that can make your business successful, as well as threats that might cause it to fail. In this section of your business plan, you will analyze the overall industry and market trends that shape the way your products and services are produced and purchased. This section provides an overview of your competition and customers that will be followed later on by further analysis of direct competitors and target customers.

Start by analyzing the structure of your industry, including the competition, the technology, and barriers to entering and exiting the industry. Next look at the markets and determine their total size, their growth potential, and the different products and services available to consumers. Then review the flow of products and services from producer to consumer. Finally, study the cost structure of the industry.

Ideally, you will want to show readers of your business plan that you are in a growth industry that is being fueled by continuing market demand. Make sure you cite reliable sources, such as government agencies, trade associations, business publications, and general newspapers as you describe the industry and market trends.

Also, don't be afraid to recognize any factors that might be stumbling blocks for your own business. These must be pointed out as risk factors to potential lenders and investors and addressed through contingencies in your business plan.

Industry structure

One of the key characteristics of an industry is the number of competitors. Think of the automobile industry in relation to the restaurant industry. You can literally count the number of automobile manufacturers on your fingers, while you would need a calculator to add up all of the restaurants. For your business plan, you will want to identify whether the structure of your industry has only one competitor (a monopoly), a few large competitors (an oligopoly), or has too many competitors to list individually (highly competitive).

In addition to counting the number of competitors in your industry, you should create a list of the major competitors in terms of sales revenue, units produced, profits, and number of employees. If you are in a highly competitive industry, where there are too many competitors to list individually, list the top 50 using the same criteria mentioned previously.

Use the following example for the automobile industry to get you started.

Automobile industry	Sales ($millions)	Units (thousands)	Profits ($millions)	Employees (thousands)
General Motors	$178,184	5,536	$6,598	632
Ford	$145,368	4,240	$5,848	345
Chrysler	$61,157	3,204	$2,705	124

In addition to listing the major competitors in your industry, try to obtain other industry information from sources such as government agencies, trade associations, business publications, and general newspapers. For instance, the following is a description of the retail industry made available by the International Trade Administration.

Description of the retail industry

(Source: International Trade Administration, http://www.ita.doc.gov)

♦ The retail industry is one of the largest industries in the United States. In 1995, retail sales reached $2.3 trillion.

♦ The retail industry is one of the largest employers in the United States, employing more than 20 million people in 1995—nearly one out of every five employed persons works in the retail industry.

♦ Between 1994 and 2005, it is projected by the Department of Labor that the retail industry will create 2.3 to 3.0 million jobs.

♦ In 1994, there were more than 1.4 million retail establishments, which are predominately small businesses. In 1992, 98.6 percent of all retail establishments employed less than 100 employees.

♦ Because of consumer pressure to keep prices low, retailers are very innovative in adapting new methods and implementing new technologies to reduce costs and improve service.

Industry growth rate

Another key statistic that readers of your business plan will be looking for is the industry growth rate. The growth rate is important because new businesses have a better chance of succeeding in an industry that is growing rapidly, rather than one that is growing only moderately or not at all.

A sample industry and market analysis

South Mill competes in the growing market for casual dress clothes in the apparel industry. According to the Current Industrial Reports published by the U.S. Department of Commerce, industry shipments of polo shirts and T-shirts increased from $5.9 billion in 1995 to $6.3 billion in 1996, or by nearly 7 percent. For this same period, the value of shipments for men's polo shirts and T-shirts increased from $4.3 billion to $4.4 billion, or by 2 percent, while for women it increased from $1.5 billion to $1.9 billion, or by nearly 27 percent.

Description	1996 Units Thousands	1996 Value $Millions	1996 Units Thousands	1995 Value $Millions
Men's				
• Woven sport shirts	22,833	$255.1	24,769	$246.4
• Knit T-shirts	916,335	4,174.1	863,032	4,073.6
Subtotal	939,168	4,429.2	887,801	4,320.0
Women's				
• Woven sport shirts	102,386	814.5	81,292	631.9
• Knit T-shirts	243,526	1,104.2	174,630	914.8
Subtotal	345,912	1,918.7	255,922	1,546.7
Grand total	1,285,080	6,347.9	1,143,723	5,866.7

The growth of the polo shirt and T-shirt segments of the apparel industry can be attributed to several factors. First, the trends to become more physically fit and dressing more casually for work and social activities have made it acceptable for this type of clothing to be worn as daily attire. Second, the versatility of cotton fabric, in conjunction with advances in technology and manufacturing, have improved clothing design and quality, resulting in higher customer demand. Lastly, because the basic styles of polo shirts and T-shirts are not driven by fads or trends in fashion, consumer demand stays relatively stable.

As in most industries, consumers continually want more value for their money, including higher quality and greater variety at the same or lower prices. Consumers want polo shirts and T-shirts that last longer, come in a variety of colors, and are comfortable enough to wear all day.

Recently, the channels of distribution to reach customers have become more diversified. In the past, polo shirts and T-shirts were distributed mainly through specialty clothing and department stores. Today, however, these articles of clothing can be purchased through mail order catalogs, mass merchandisers, the Internet, and other channels of distribution. The growing number of distribution channels has given manufacturers the opportunity to serve more customers with a wider range of products.

In order to meet these demands, manufacturers have had to adjust their business strategies to remain competitive. To address the consumer need for better quality at the same price, producers have upgraded their manufacturing processes by using newer technology and machinery. Further, to satisfy an increasing number of customers created by the new channels of distribution, manufacturers have had to become more flexible in their product development and production methods.

Look at the industry and market analysis for South Mill, and note that the company establishes how large the industry for polo shirts and T-shirts is—$6.3 billion—and how fast it is growing—nearly 7 percent annually—by using industry output information provided by the U.S. Department of Commerce. The South Mill plan then goes on to explain how the market trends, such as dressing more casually for work, are driving the market.

Technology

Most industries are technology-driven. However, technology has a greater influence in some industries than in others. The computer industry is very reliant on changes in technology that occur in software development and chip design. As software becomes more efficient and chips become faster, computer manufacturers must incorporate these underlying changes into their products. If a computer manufacturer fails to keep up with the latest developments in technology, it will be overrun by the competition.

For your business plan, identify any relevant technology that might have a bearing on your future. Explain how you will use this technology to your benefit and how it will keep you ahead of the competition. Also, if you are aware of any technology changes in the future, explain how you will incorporate them into your business.

Barriers to entering and exiting an industry

Is it more difficult to make a car or a hamburger? Although the answer is obvious, the reasoning as to why it is more difficult to make a car than a hamburger tells you a lot about the barriers to entering and exiting an industry. To manufacture a car, you need to purchase a large factory, fill it with the latest machinery, and hire many skilled people. Conversely, to make a hamburger, you simply need to purchase a grill and hire a cook. The investment and resources required to produce a car are significantly greater than those required to cook a hamburger, and make it more difficult for new competitors to enter the automobile manufacturing industry than the restaurant industry.

The ease or difficulty with which competitors can enter an industry are termed *entry barriers*. Entry barriers include not only large capital outlays, but also government regulation, availability of skilled personnel, established channels of distribution, and anything else that might keep competitors out of your industry.

Exit barriers, on the other hand, indicate how difficult it is for a competitor to leave the industry. Exit barriers may be the same as entry barriers, only for a different set of reasons. For example, if you have financed your business using outside resources, such as banks or venture capitalists, it may be very difficult for you to convince these investors that they should abandon their investments because you don't want to be in business anymore.

Market size and growth

Industries live and die by the markets they serve. It is still possible for your business to be successful in a slow-growing industry, as long as you are a small competitor serving a very large market, or you are able to meet the needs of a rapidly growing market. For instance, many of the PC manufacturers that now have household names, such as Dell and Gateway, were at one time tiny competitors in the very large computer industry. However, because of the rapid growth of the PC market and their ability to capitalize on the trend for mail order, these companies have become very successful (and also very large) in the past 10 years.

Although large or rapidly growing markets can be an excellent opportunity for your business, they will also attract plenty of competitors. Larger competitors in your industry, as well as new entrants, will try to squeeze you out of the market by duplicating your success. Therefore, it is important that your business plan provides an adequate description of how you will be able to cope with the competition and, at the same time, satisfy the needs of the market.

Market trends

There are many underlying market trends that can affect your industry. For instance, South Mill notes that the general trend of the population to become more physically fit is having a positive influence on its business of producing polo shirts and T-shirts. Some other trends that might influence your market include:

♦ Aging of the "baby boomer" generation.

♦ Increasing anti-smoking sentiment.

♦ More families with both parents working.

♦ Desire of people to live longer, healthier lives.

♦ More employees working at home.

New trends seem to be spotted almost daily by economists and market researchers. For your business plan, identify any market trends that might have a positive or negative influence on your business. Explain how your business can capitalize on positive market trends and what contingencies you have for negative market trends.

Product and service characteristics

It's worthwhile for you to note any product and service characteristics that are unique to your industry. You stand a much better chance of success if you can differentiate your products and services from the rest of the competitors in your industry. Product differentiation becomes increasingly difficult for commodity-type products such as gasoline, phone service, or poultry, and the markets for these products are often driven by price considerations.

One way to analyze the product and service characteristics of your industry is to examine the offerings of the largest competitors. Do their products and services have unique characteristics that might make them appeal to different markets? Think of the fast-food industry and how some of the largest competitors have differentiated their products. Burger King has differentiated itself through its cooking process (flame broiling), while Taco Bell has settled on offering something completely different than hamburgers (tacos).

Flow of products and services

Think of your industry as being analogous to a railway line. There is a train track that runs between a supply of raw materials and the final consumer, with a series of stops along the way. At each stop, or station, the freight is unloaded, processed, and then reloaded until it finally reaches the consumer in the desired form. For instance, think of all the stops a tomato must make before arriving at your door on top of a pizza. It goes from the tomato farmer, to the food-processing factory, to a warehouse (inside a can), to a pizza parlor, and then finally to your home.

Once you can visualize your industry in this format, then you will have a better understanding of how your entire industry operates. Further, you will be able to identify potential trouble spots along the way and note other areas offering new opportunities. Consider your business as being one of the train stations on the railway line, where you add value to freight that is unloaded and then send it on its way to the next station.

As you conduct this analysis, highlight any potential supply problems that you might encounter. Is there an adequate supply of raw materials for your business? Are there multiple suppliers? Is your supply of raw materials competitively priced? Is your supply of raw materials subject to fluctuating prices?

On the departing side of your business, note whether any of your distribution channels are subject to failure. Do you have more than one channel of distribution? How much control does your channel of distribution have over the pricing of your products? Can your channel of distribution affect the quality of your products? How much influence does your channel of distribution have over the consumer to make product choices?

Ideally, you would like to be in an industry that has multiple suppliers and allows you to reach consumers through multiple channels of distribution. If this is not the case, make sure you have some contingencies for your business plan. There is nothing more discouraging than having an empty warehouse because you can't get supplies, or having a full warehouse because you can't make deliveries.

Cost structure

As you conduct your industry analysis, you will undoubtedly come across objectives from other businesses that state, "We plan to become the low-cost producer in our industry." If your competitors have a significantly lower cost structure than your business, then they will have the opportunity to charge lower prices for their products and services and drive you out of the market. As you enter an industry, you will want to ensure that your cost structure is similar to that of your major competitors.

Cost structure is best defined as the cost per unit produced. For every unit of product that you produce, you will have certain variable and fixed costs (see the section on breakeven analysis in Chapter 10, Finances). The level of these costs can be determined by such factors as efficient machinery, purchasing power, and the length of time a business has been in the industry.

To see how your business will match up on cost structure with other competitors in your industry, simply ask yourself whether you can make a profit by selling your products at the established market price. Look at the gross profit margin (cost of goods sold ÷ sales revenue) of other competitors in your industry, and see if you will at least be able to operate in this range. If not, then it will be very difficult for your business to be competitive in the industry.

In summary, the "Industry and Market Analysis" section of your business plan provides a general description of your competitors and customers. It addresses the number and type of competitors in your industry, how fast they are growing, and the barriers to entering and exiting the industry. It will also identify the total size of the market, its growth rate, and any underlying trends that can have an effect on demand for your products and services.

Chapter 5

Customers

Questions to be answered in this chapter:

♦ How many potential customers are in your target market?

♦ What is your share of this market?

♦ What do they buy from your business? How much do they buy?

♦ What key variables can you use to separate them into groups?

♦ How are you going to retain existing customers?

The number of customers that your business will satisfy drives every aspect of your business plan. Customers determine your level of sales and profits, the number of people you will need to hire, where your business will be located, how much financing you will require, and how long you will be in business. Therefore, it is imperative that your market research clearly identifies your ideal customers.

Readers of your business plan will want to know: Who are your customers? Where are they located? How many of them are there? What are their unique characteristics? What do they buy from your business? In an ideal world you would personally describe every customer and create a marketing plan tailored to each individual's needs. However, unless your target market is extremely small, you will need to think of your customers as larger groups sharing similar characteristics.

Customers and market segmentation

Regardless of whether your plan involves starting a business with only prospective customers or expanding an existing business with an established customer base, you will need to segment your market. Market segmentation is the process of dividing your market into smaller, more manageable groups of customers (or prospects for a new business) with similar needs or behavior patterns. For instance, a diaper manufacturer might choose to segment the market by identifying "all parents with children under the age of three." This manufacturer could, of course, take the segmentation further by separating "children" into "boys and girls" and then "boys between the ages of 18 and 36 months."

Market segmentation requires that you identify customer differences based on your product offerings and match them with descriptive information such as demographics, customer, size, business type, geography, or psychographics. An owner of a movie theater showing multiple titles could segment customers by viewing preference (comedy, drama, or action) or by age group (child, teenager, or adult).

Imagine if the diaper manufacturer or movie theater owner did not incorporate market segmentation into his or her respective business plan. He or she would be hunting for needles in a haystack. The diaper manufacturer might spend millions of dollars on an advertising campaign that only reached a few parents with young children. The movie theater owner might start showing movies made for a teenage audience in a town filled with empty nesters. Even by using one of the simplest forms of segmentation, such as demographics, these businesses can increase their chances of success.

Demographic segmentation is one of the simplest and most widely used forms of market segmentation. By using demographics, you can target specific groups of customers or businesses. Demographic variables for consumer markets include age, race, gender, occupation, and income level. For business-to-business marketing, consider number of employees, type of business (manufacturing, merchandising, or service), sales revenue, or business structure (proprietorship, partnership, or corporation).

There are many ways to segment your markets and create groups of potential customers. The following table summarizes the most common forms of segmentation.

Type of Segmentation	Market Segments	Example
Demographic	Age, gender, income, occupation, race, family size, or religion	A lipstick manufacturer would use gender (female) as a market segment
Psychographic	Needs, motives, perceptions, attitudes, or reference groups	Diet plans target individuals who want to lose weight
Product or Service	Benefits or usage	Phone companies segment on monthly long distance charges.
Geographic	Urban, suburban, rural, or climate	Suntan lotion distributors gauge distribution by climate.

A great way for you to begin your market segmentation is to look at some of the demographic variables used by direct marketing companies, such as American List Counsel or Database America. These businesses compile mailing lists, for sale, using some of the following demographics:

Example consumer segments:

- Mortgage information
- Pet owners
- Marital status
- Credit card holders
- Gender
- Ethnic group
- Occupation
- Homeowner

Example business segments:

- Annual sales
- Standard Industrial Classification (SIC)
- Job title
- Hotels by number of rooms
- Churches by denomination
- Truck by fleet size
- Attorneys by specialty
- Site information

To locate these companies and learn more, see the section on secondary market research in Chapter 6, Market Research.

Retaining existing customers

Satisfying and retaining customers is the key to success for any business. By selling your existing customers as many products and services as possible, you will increase their loyalty to your business, build long-term rewarding relationships, and close out the competition.

As you begin to think about your current customers, try to categorize them in simple terms.

My best customers:

- Drive sports cars.
- Spend between $50 and $100 a month on phone service.
- Subscribe to computer magazines.
- Drink a case of beer every week.
- Eat gourmet food.
- Have a college education.
- Live in high-rise apartments.

By describing your customers in these terms, you have begun to segment the market. One of the most important ways you can segment your existing business is by analyzing the monthly purchases of your customers. Simply make a list that starts with the customer who spends the most with your business and end with the one who spends the least. In the following table Customer A would spend the most with your business, and Customer E would spend the least.

Customer	Monthly purchases from your business	Monthly purchases from your competition	Total monthly purchases
A	$2,000	$0	$2,000
B	$1,000	$500	$1,500
C	$500	$1,000	$1,500
D	$500	$2,000	$2,500
E	$200	$300	$500

With this type of analysis, you have segmented your customers by the amount they spend with your business.

Take the segmentation one step further by including the total monthly purchases your customers make from both your business and the competition. For example, although Customer D spends only $500 on your products and services, he spends a total of $2,500 when you include purchases from the competition.

Now you can begin to develop a marketing strategy based on the segmentation analysis. For instance you could do either of the following:

♦ Target prospects who spend more than $1,000 per month on the types of products and services you offer.

♦ Target prospects who spend more than $500 per month with the competition.

Market segmentation means focusing on a particular niche of a market that will be profitable for your business. This depends on choosing the right segment, with the right product and image to satisfy your prospects' needs. Finally, segmentation has to be constantly reexamined because the characteristics of the market constantly change as new customers enter and old ones leave.

Market size and share

After you have described your ideal customer groups using market segmentation, you will want to tell readers of your business plan about the size of the potential market. The size of the overall market, and your share, is important because it provides a gauge for how large your business can become. If you can satisfy millions of customers with your products and services, but you have little or no market share, your business has a large growth potential. Conversely, if you are in a small market and have a large market share, your prospects for growth are limited.

Think of market size and share in terms of a pizza pie. The size of the pie—8 inches, 12 inches, or 16 inches—is analogous to the size of your market, and the number of slices comparable to your market share. For example, the market size and share of the Big Three U.S. auto makers might be broken down as follows:

	General Motors	Ford	Chrysler	Total
Number of cars and trucks	1,384,000	1,060,000	801,100	3,245,100
Market share	42.6%	32.7%	24.7%	100%

In this example the size of the pie is 3,245,100 cars and trucks, with GM having a little more than 4 slices, Ford having just over 3 slices, and Chrysler with nearly 2.5 slices (in a 10-slice pie).

Make sure that you express market share in terms of units and dollars. In some markets, it is possible for a business to have a small share of the units sold and a higher share of the total dollar value. If the preceding example were expanded to include the entire U.S. automotive market, with other manufacturers such as Rolls Royce, BMW, and Range Rover, the number of units sold would increase, as would the dollar value of the market. On closer examination, you would find that luxury auto makers have a lower share of the units sold relative to their higher share of the total dollar value of the market.

Chapter 6

Market Research

Questions to be answered in this chapter:

- ◆ What competitors do your prospects consider when evaluating alternatives?
- ◆ Do your prospective customers have a contract with a competitor?
- ◆ What are your customer preferences for color, styling, service levels, and payment?
- ◆ Why did your prospects choose a competitor?
- ◆ How much do your competitors charge for their products and services?

Market research is divided into two categories: primary market research and secondary market research. Secondary market research makes use of existing news sources, trade statistics, databases, and general knowledge to help you answer questions such as: "What is the potential sales revenue for the product?"or "How many prospects and customers are in this market?" Because secondary market research is inexpensive and readily accessible, you will want to exhaust all of these sources before considering primary market research.

After reviewing all of the secondary market research sources, you may still have some unanswered questions about your customers, competitors, markets, or products and services. To get answers to these questions, you might consider primary market research. However, because primary market research is time-consuming and expensive, it is important that you have narrowed your market with secondary research.

Primary market research requires direct contact with potential customers of your product or service. You collect data from the marketplace through mail surveys, Internet questionnaires, telephone interviews, focus groups, or mall intercepts. For instance, you may want to ask your potential customers why they purchased a particular product or service (was it the color, packaging, service level, or price?).

Secondary market research

Secondary market research makes use of existing news sources, trade statistics, databases, and general knowledge to help you determine:

- ♦ What is the potential sales revenue for your product?
- ♦ How many prospects and customers are in this market?
- ♦ Who are the largest competitors in the market?
- ♦ What market segment do they serve?
- ♦ How many competitors are in your potential market?
- ♦ What types of services and products does the competition offer?

It is called secondary market research because you obtain the information "second-hand," or from an intermediary source, and not directly from the market. A good example of some secondary market research that you have performed in the past would be a trip to the library where you searched through books and magazines and then prepared a report for school. For your business plan, you also will need to collect data from existing sources of information, such as trade journals, business publications, newspapers, and industry related books.

One of the best ways to start your secondary market research is by contacting companies that gather and compile lists, such as:

American List Counsel Inc.

88 Orchard Road, CN-5219
Princeton, NJ 08543
908-874-4300
Fax: 908-874-4433
Internet: http://www.amlist.com

Database America Companies

100 Paragon Drive
Montvale, NJ 07645-0419
800-223-7777 or 201-476-2300
Fax: 201-476-2419
Internet: http://www.databaseamerica.com

Both of these companies publish excellent catalogs with a complete breakdown of the types of lists they offer. For instance, American List Counsel publishes more than 10,000 mailing lists, one of which is a list of "consumers who have purchased collectibles, fashions, gifts, and other products from more than 100 Warner Bros. Studio Stores nationwide."

Database America also has many specialized lists, such as: women- and minority-owned businesses, franchise owners, affluent households, and a pet owners database. Some lists can be broken down to sales volume by state or professional title by state.

Although one of the main reasons businesses purchase these lists is to generate sales leads, they are also an excellent resource for conducting secondary market research.

Estimating the potential sales revenue for a given market is as much art as it is science. If you do your homework, go to the library, check out the Internet, and read articles in your selected area of interest, you will get an excellent idea of the total potential sales revenue in your market.

In addition to estimating sales revenue, you will want to review industry conditions and trends, the competition, and new product and service offerings on the horizon. Some tips for gathering secondary market research include:

- Subscribe to a least one general business publication, such as *BusinessWeek, Forbes,* or *Fortune.* If you can afford it, order all three. These magazines will give you a feel for the current state of your selected industry, as well as what to expect in the future.

- Subscribe to a trade publication specific to your chosen industry. Study the commentary and advertising for product features and new releases.

- Join your industry organization.

- Go to the library and review the *U.S. Industrial Outlook,* published by the U.S. Department of Commerce. It provides in-depth analysis of more than 50 industries from aerospace to wood products.

- Call or write to your competitors and ask for their brochures and sales literature. Make a list of benefits advertised by your competition and decide how you will differentiate your product or service.

- Explore the Internet.

Sizing the market

If you are starting a new business, secondary market research will help you estimate the potential sales revenue for your product or service. This market can be estimated by multiplying the potential unit volume by an average selling price.

There are literally hundreds of "unit" measurements in the United States, so you should evaluate yours carefully. Units can be expressed in terms of number of buildings, people, households, job titles, buyers, square feet, and so on.

Let's say you are considering the introduction of a new pocket calculator designed for engineers. American List Counsel has mailing lists for both engineers and engineering firms. For 1997, it lists 275,201 engineers with counts by specialty (air pollution, geological, mining and mineral, etc). Also, you know from experience that scientific pocket calculators sell for between $25 and $75 each and tend to last for five years.

Estimates for the low and high potential yearly sales revenue would be:

$$(275,201/5) * \$25 = \$1,376,005$$

$$(275,201/5) * \$75 = \$4,128,015$$

With these estimates, you have begun to gauge the total market but still need to investigate other factors, such as: "Does this list contain all engineers or is this only a segment that responded to a survey?" and "What is the potential market share for a new entrant in this business?"

Once you have exhausted the secondary market research sources, such as list companies, trade journals, business publications, the library, and the Internet, then it is time to consider some primary market research.

Primary market research

Primary market research requires direct contact with potential customers of your product or service and may be conducted through mail surveys, telephone interviews, focus groups, mall intercepts, or Internet forms.

Example of primary market research

Genuine Pizza, Inc., noticed that sales had fallen by more than 10 percent for the past three months compared to the previous year. The owner was concerned because the number of potential customers in his neighborhood had actually increased during this time. Some simple primary research revealed the problem.

Because part of Genuine Pizza's business included home deliveries, there was plenty of opportunity for direct customer contact. When a customer called the store to place an order, the owner asked if he could follow up the next day for some feedback. The follow-up call consisted of a few simple questions:

◆ Was your pizza "hot" when it was delivered?
◆ How was the pizza? Too much sauce? Not enough?
◆ Did it arrive on time?
◆ Do you have any other comments about Genuine Pizza?

At the end of the week, the owner began to notice a trend that some customers were very satisfied with Genuine Pizza, while others were thoroughly dissatisfied. There did not seem to be a middle ground.

A little more investigation revealed that the customers who were dissatisfied with Genuine Pizza had received deliveries from the same individual. It turned out that one of Genuine Pizza's employees was not very courteous when delivering pizza! Horn blowing seemed to be part of the problem.

The owner fixed his personnel problem by hiring another driver and he restored some loyalty with his dissatisfied customers by sending them a coupon for a free pizza.

Researching customer losses

For an existing business, your primary market research should begin with departing customers. Losing customers will reduce your profits, increase your marketing expenses, and lower your cash flow. Therefore, it is important that you learn why customers are leaving your business and implement changes to retain them. Primary market research will provide you with the information you need.

◆ The first step is to define "lost" customers. These are not only customers who leave your business entirely for the competition, but also those who shift part of their purchases to an alternate source.

◆ Next you must identify which customers have been lost. This list should be broken down by customer size (how much they purchased from your company) prior to moving business to the competition.

◆ Categorize the reasons the customers left your business. These will include service, price, quality, and distribution alternatives.

◆ Finally, have a third party interview your departing customers to determine exactly why they left. These interviews can be conducted over the phone or in person, but should be as specific as possible. For example, customers don't leave because your price was too high, they leave because the competition "offered a 25-percent discount on the first full year of business, followed by a 15-percent discount on each successive year."

Length of the survey or questionnaire

Because primary research relies heavily on customer feedback, you must be sensitive to how you approach your customers or prospective customers. You don't want to pester or alienate them.

If you are using a survey or questionnaire, you should bear in mind that there is a trade-off between the quantity of data collected and the quality. If you try to ask too many questions, you will not get many completed surveys. If you don't ask enough questions, then you won't know if your idea will be successful.

The appropriate survey length depends upon the importance of the subject to the respondent. Some purchases, such as a telephone system or home, are so important to consumers that a four-page survey is reasonable. Other purchases, such as coffee or a magazine, are so routine that more than four or five questions would be too many.

Your rule of thumb is to ask as few questions as possible, and still get the answers you need. If you don't need a piece of information, such as "How many years have you lived in Altoona?" don't ask! Only ask questions that will help you determine if your idea will be successful.

The manner in which you ask your prospects and customers questions will also determine your success. If you schedule an appointment, provide lunch, and indicate that the survey will take no more than 45 minutes to complete, you will have a much higher completion rate than if you blindly mail a 15-page survey to someone who has never heard of you or your company.

Tips to increase your response rate

To maximize your response rate, keep the following tips in mind:

- Keep the survey short. Long surveys are time-consuming and can be rejected by potential respondents.
- Make the survey user-friendly. Use check boxes wherever possible and maximize the amount of "white space" in the survey. Leave space for the respondent to make comments or special remarks.
- Offer an incentive for completing and returning the survey, such as discount coupons or a free meal.
- If there is no incentive, such as "free movie tickets," enclose a postage-paid return envelope.
- Use an up-to-date mailing list. If you are not using your own list, then find out how and when these individuals were last contacted. Were they called? Did they renew their magazine subscriptions? As a list increases with age, you can expect a poorer response rate.
- Send a cover letter. The letter should come from the highest-ranking individual in your organization and should tell the respondent the importance of his or her opinion.
- Send a follow-up mailing. A postcard with a brief reminder message can be sent two weeks following the original questionnaire mailing.

A budget for market research

In the evaluation of a business opportunity, you must consider the amount of money that will be required to research the idea. Secondary market research is inexpensive and can be conducted rapidly, while primary market research is expensive and can be time-consuming.

The following is a full-blown market research plan, with cost estimates for "out-of-pocket" expenses. These estimates exclude any costs associated with your time for reading and evaluating the research.

Type of research	Description of research	Estimated cost
Secondary	Subscribe to a general business publication, such as *BusinessWeek* or *Forbes*.	$50 - $75
Secondary	Subscribe to an industry specific publication, such as a trade journal (many trade journals are free).	Free - $100
Secondary	Internet service	$20/month

Primary	• Mail 2,000 surveys or questionnaires
	  • Mailing piece should be $0.60 with postage and prospect name from list provider
	  • With a 10-percent response rate, and a $5 incentive
		$1,200
		
		$1,000

Primary	Call 2,000 prospects • With a 15-percent response rate and a 5-minute interview	$1,500
Primary	Conduct focus groups in New York, Los Angeles, Chicago, and Miami (2 per city, or 8 total)	$32,000

At a minimum, a full-blown marketing research project can easily exceed $30,000 if you include direct mail, telemarketing, and focus groups.

For smaller businesses, it is virtually impossible to justify such a large market research expense. This may be more than you expect to sell in your first year of operation! Therefore, you should rely heavily on the secondary market research, but still attempt to do some primary market research. Even if you mail 200 surveys and receive 20 responses, you will have gained some valuable insight into your prospective market.

In larger enterprises, where the risks are much greater, it would be an oversight not to conduct a full-blown market research project. Consider the introduction of a new automobile that may cost billions of dollars. The expense of conducting $30,000 or even $100,000 in market research is minimal when compared to missing out on an important product attribute that may help you sell more new cars.

Interviewing executives

Your target for most surveys is the decision-maker. This can either be the head of a household, a vice president of research and development, or the president of a corporation. If you are trying to interview a corporate decision-maker, you will face a different set of barriers than if you are attempting to reach the head of a household. Executives are often hard to reach and are frequently asked to complete surveys.

A good idea is to try to establish a relationship between your company and that of the individual you wish to interview. If your company is already selling products to the targeted executive's company, then you have an established relationship. If you or your business are unknown to the executive, try using a reference from a mutual business acquaintance or a friend. Many times, you can overcome the lack of a relationship by offering an incentive, such as promising to provide the results of the survey or one of your products for free.

As a last resort, you can offer money in exchange for the interview. To add credibility, you may ask the executive if he or she would like to donate it to a charity of their choice. Make sure that the person conducting the interview has an in-depth knowledge of the industry. This will ensure that the executive feels that he or she is being surveyed by another industry professional and can address any unique concerns. Also, be sure to schedule your interview in advance and confirm on the day before the appointment. You should also establish a time limit to be no more than an hour, preferably about 15 minutes. This holds true for both in-person and telephone interviews.

The format for your interview should include as many open-ended questions as possible to encourage the executive to provide as much information as possible about the chosen subject. For instance, ask, "Which departments and management levels are normally involved in a purchasing decision?" Keep close-ended questions to a minimum. Don't ask, "Do the engineering manager and purchasing agent make all of the buying decisions?"

Chapter 7

Competition

Questions to be answered in this chapter:

- ♦ Who are your direct and indirect competitors?
- ♦ How large are your competitors in sales and in profits?
- ♦ What are your competitor segments?
- ♦ How is your business better than theirs?
- ♦ What are the weaknesses of your direct competitors?

It is not unrealistic for you to base your entire business plan around what other competitors in your industry are doing. Based upon your idea, you could simply study the marketing, management, and finances of one (or a few) of your direct competitors and develop a comprehensive business plan. However, instead of developing a "me-too" plan, you will want to describe everything that differentiates your business from your direct competitors, makes it superior, and will cause customers to select your products and services over theirs.

The thought process that you will use to develop this section of your business plan is similar in many respects to that described previously for developing customer segments. If there are many competitors in your industry, then you will want to group them into direct and indirect competitors. For instance, if you were going to open a fast-food restaurant then your direct competitors would be other fast food restaurants, and your indirect competitors would be sandwich shops, a diner or two, and any other establishments that sell prepared food.

Sometimes it will not be clear who your direct and indirect competitors are until you conduct some market research. Remember how you answered the "What business am I in?" question. If you owned a movie theater, then you might have answered the question by saying, "I am in the movie theater business," and you would only consider other movie theaters as your direct competitors. However, think about who your competitors would be if you had answered the question by saying, "I am in the entertainment business."

All of a sudden, you are not only competing with other movie theaters, but also with video game arcades, video rental stores, cable television, and any other businesses selling consumer entertainment.

Many businesses make the mistake of entering markets that are already saturated with competitors. These markets tend to have been established for a period of time, and most, if not all, of the customers' needs are being satisfied. Analyzing the competition will help you to identify a market niche that is not saturated, where you can compete effectively and satisfy the needs of your customers.

Studying the competition

Readers of your business plan will want to know all about your competition. Who they are? How many of them are there? Is their business increasing or decreasing? How is your business different and better than theirs? Look for opportunities where your business can gain a competitive advantage. Capitalize on their weaknesses and avoid their strengths. Take the following steps:

- Prepare a list of all of your competitors, including name, address, phone, e-mail, etc.
- Review their advertisements and brochures, and summarize their product features and benefits.
- Study their pricing strategies and determine what value they are offering customers.
- Determine if they are trying to hire or lay people off. Who are they trying to hire or fire?
- Call them on the telephone and listen to their greetings and to how your questions are answered.
- Visit their stores and buy their products.
- Go to a trade show and get one of their brochures.
- Try returning something you bought from one of your competitors. Could you return an item only for credit or could you get your money back?

By conducting a thorough study of your competition, you will be able to learn what business tasks they perform well. For instance, a PC retailer might review the competitive practices of PC mail order companies and discover that providing technical support over the phone is a perceived benefit by new computer buyers. If the PC retailer were to incorporate technical phone support into its existing operation, it would gain a competitive advantage over other PC retailers without technical support, and would be on a "level playing field" with PC mail order companies.

Segmenting the competition

After you have made a list of all of your possible competitors, you should group or segment them to identify who you are really competing against. Competitors can be segmented according to the markets they serve, the products they produce, or their business operations.

Once you have completed your market segmentation and identified your target customers, then you might identify your direct competitors as those who are serving the same market. For instance, suppose your business plan calls for selling your products and services to high-income families. Identify your competitors as those who are selling similar products and services to this market. To facilitate this process, consider using some of the demographic variables discussed previously. For example, an upscale hotel might consider its direct competitors to be other hotels that cater to families with incomes in excess of $100,000 per year.

The most obvious way to segment your competitors is according to the products and services they produce. You can consider your competitors to be those who produce the same or similar products and services as your business. However, just because you are selling products and services that are similar to those of another business, does not mean that you are actually in competition with that business. Customers make the decision. Think about a large multinational corporation in search of an advertising agency. This corporation will consider only a handful of the larger agencies to handle its account and rule out the myriad of smaller agencies that essentially provide the same services.

Along the same lines as looking at the products and services that other businesses offer, you can also look at their operations to determine if they are your competitors. Competitors can be grouped according to their production capabilities, research and development personnel, product and service variety, or channels of distribution. For example, a mail-order PC business may consider other mail-order PC businesses as direct competitors, and PC retailers as indirect competitors.

There are as many ways to segment competitors as there are ways to segment customers. You must select the most appropriate criteria for your industry while considering your goals and objectives for the future. If you want to compete with Coca-Cola, then you must set goals and objectives that will make your business better than Coca-Cola.

Customer benefits offered by the competition

Although it would be great if your business could be the best at everything, economic and financial constraints will cause you to choose your battles carefully. Ideally, you will select areas where you can afford to compete, where the competition is weak, and where customers will perceive a benefit. Create a table similar to the following and map your business to the competition.

Competitor name	Customer benefit	Do you offer this benefit?	If no, how much would it cost to do so
	Low prices		
	Diverse product line		
	Excellent customer service		
	High quality		
	Extended warranty		
	Different financing options		

Below is South Mill's description of the competition. Note that the company has identified its direct competitors by name and also placed itself in the industry by describing their relative sizes. Its supporting material would include the annual sales revenue and unit volumes for these competitors.

A sample description of the competition

The market for polo shirts and T-shirts is very competitive. South Mill's major competitors are also vertically integrated manufacturers and include many larger businesses, such as Sara Lee, Russell, and Fruit of the Loom, and smaller job-shop type operations, including Truvalt West and True Shirt. In order to continue its success in this market, South Mill will maintain its focus on limited product lines (polo shirts and T-shirts) manufactured to the highest quality standards at competitive price points, and will use the most technologically advanced manufacturing processes and methods.

Chapter 8

Marketing Strategy

Questions to be answered in this chapter:

- What are your product and service benefits?
- How are you pricing your products and services?
- How will you advertise your product and service benefits?
- What are your channels of distribution?
- Where is your business located?
- How large is your marketing budget?

Marketing addresses the four "P's" of your business: product, price, promotion, and place. The combination, or mix, of these elements will define your marketing strategy. In earlier sections of your business plan, you already described your product and service benefits, and how they will meet the needs of your target customers. This section addresses how you will price your product and service benefits, how you will promote them, and how you will deliver them to your customers.

Once you have established how your product and service benefits will satisfy a prospect's needs, such as being the most economical, the fastest, or the most entertaining, you must consider an appropriate pricing strategy for these benefits. Pricing, especially for small or startup businesses, can lead to its success or failure. After all, pricing will determine the level of profits for your business, and ultimately whether it will remain solvent in the years to come.

In order to communicate your product and service benefits to your potential customers, you will need to develop a promotion and advertising strategy. This strategy involves the creation of a message that stresses your product and service benefits for your potential customers. It also takes into account the most appropriate forms of media communication, such as direct mail or print advertising, and establishes a budget for advertising expenses.

The last P in the four "P's" of marketing stands for place. Place, or your channels of distribution, describe where and how your customers will actually take possession of your products or services. If your business involves retailing, you will want to describe the location and layout of your store. If you are a direct marketer, you will want to describe your methods of transportation for delivering your products. If your business involves face-to-face selling, you will want to describe your sales force.

Effective marketing is expensive, particularly if you have to pay rent, hire a direct sales force, or do a substantial amount of advertising. Therefore it is important that you develop a realistic budget for these expenses and incorporate them into your financial management plan.

Why the low-price strategy is unappealing

Are you familiar with the term red flag? This is a term that the Internal Revenue Service (IRS) often uses when reviewing a tax return that seems unrealistic. Red flags lead to audits, which can lead to penalties, and sometimes even jail. If you would like to raise a red flag in your business plan, just say that your pricing strategy, and maybe even your whole marketing strategy, is based on having lower prices than your competition. Upon seeing this strategy, potential investors will probably run for the door and start evaluating their next opportunity.

Why is the low-price strategy unappealing to investors? Lower prices are associated with lower profits that cannot be made up with additional volume. The best place to get examples of this is the stock market. Watch a company's stock after it announces an "across-the-board price cut." Barring other factors, its stock price always lowers. Usually the converse is also true. When a company announces a price increase, its stock price rises. AOL's announcement that it was raising monthly access prices to above $20 per month was complemented with a big jump in its stock price.

If you are saying to yourself, "This doesn't apply to me because I'm not a big company and don't ever plan to have any stockholders," then you are in for a big disappointment. Not only does this apply to your company, it is even more important because you do not have the financial resources of the larger publicly traded companies. The following table shows what happens to your profits when you try to become the low-price supplier.

	Current	Beat the competition strategy (5% discount)	Increase required to maintain profits
Sales	$100	$95	$190
Costs	$90	$90	$180
Profit	$10	$5	$10
Margin	10%	5.3%	5.3%

Although you lowered prices by only 5 percent, to be priced less than the competition, profits were reduced 50 percent! In order to get your profits back up to $10, you will now have to double your sales to $190. No easy task. That is why it is often said that price decreases "flow directly through to your bottom line."

The price you charge for your products and services includes not only your expenses and profits, but also intangibles such as service level, warranties, image, and quality. All of these factors are tied together in the mind of the consumer when making a purchase decision. In a perfect world, you could assign values to these intangibles and set the price accordingly. Unfortunately, consumers can be unpredictable and a high value for one consumer can be irrelevant to another.

Pricing strategies

There are a wide range of techniques you can use to set prices, and each has its advantages and disadvantages. In order to maximize profits, it is important that you choose the right method.

Cost-plus pricing

In an ideal world, we would all use cost-plus to set our prices. With this method you simply set prices to cover your fixed and variable costs, and leave enough room for profits. Unfortunately, most customers don't care about your costs (the U.S. Government excluded), and would rather get a lower price than see you make a lot of profit. Although you cannot realistically use cost-plus to set prices, you want to make sure that the aggregate prices you charge cover costs and provide for a profit.

Competitive pricing

Most markets that you have considered entering have some established pricing. Competitive pricing compares alternative products and services and sets prices accordingly. For example, the following are comparative prices for PCs.

	ABC Co.	XYZ Inc.	AAA PC	Lo-Cost PC
Processor	233 Mhz	266 Mhz	233 Mhz	200 Mhz
Memory	48 Mb	32 Mb	32 Mb	32 Mb
Hard drive	4.0 Gb	4.3 Gb	3.2 Gb	2.1 Gb
CD-ROM	24X	24X	20X	16X
Modem	56K	56K	56K	56K
Monitor	13.2"	13.8"	No	No
Printer	Yes	Yes	No	No
Zip Drive	Yes	No	No	No
Price	$1,349.70	$1,299.99	$949.99	$799.99

From this table, you can see that the computer with the least amount of features has the lowest price. However, there is not quite as much distinction between the two most expensive computers. While ABC Co. offers a Zip drive and 16 Mb more memory, its processor is slower than XYZ Inc.'s and its monitor is smaller.

By using competitive pricing, you can establish price ranges for products and services. Additionally, you can compare features, warranties, and service levels to determine premium and discount levels relative to competing products and services.

Premium pricing

Can you think of a business where you receive the same utility (an economics term meaning usefulness received by consumers), but at greatly differing prices? The lodging industry comes to mind. Most hotels provide a bed to sleep in at night and a shower for the morning, yet the prices charged for this utility can differ by 100 percent, or more. Through a well-implemented strategy of higher service levels and image building, some hotels are able to obtain premium prices over their competitors.

Some of the ways other businesses are able to achieve premium prices include:

+ Restaurants: higher quality food.
+ Hotels: better service levels.
+ Automobiles: superior performance.
+ Retail outlets: extended warranties.
+ Apparel stores: latest fashions.

If you are thinking of pursuing a premium pricing strategy, there are three key points to keep in mind: 1) Customers must perceive the value of your premium service; 2) they must be willing to pay for it; and 3) it must cost you less than the price you receive. To the last point, "do not offer gold-plated service if you are only going to receive silver-plated prices."

Cream-skimming pricing

Cream skimming is another pricing strategy that is used extensively in the high-tech markets. When a manufacturer introduces a new product, the price is initially set at a high level. Over time, as the new product becomes more widely accepted, the price is gradually reduced. Again, the PC market offers an excellent example. As every new generation of faster processor is brought to market, prices of the older processors are gradually reduced to make them more widely available. This allows the manufacturer to recover its development costs at the beginning of the sales cycle.

This strategy can work well in markets where the product or service is truly new or innovative, since it is always easier to lower prices than to raise them. In any market, you will find customers who want to be the "first on the block" with the latest product or service, and are willing to pay a premium for it. These consumers are called "early adopters." Because early adopters are price insensitive, you can use them to your advantage by initially setting prices at a high level, and then lowering them over time to increase your market share. Consider a new restaurant in town that has a line outside its door. The proprietor of this new restaurant could certainly deploy a cream-skimming strategy and charge higher prices until the line shortens.

Market-penetration pricing

This is the strategy of initially, setting prices below the competition to attract new customers. As stated at the beginning of this section, if you are planning to deploy this strategy, you will be raising a red flag for your potential investors or management. Pricing lower than the current market indicates that the most important benefit you have is low prices! Also, keep in mind that a plan to raise prices after an introductory period is difficult, because it is always easier to lower prices than to raise them.

Promotion and advertising

Once you have identified your product and service benefits and created a pricing strategy, it's time to develop an advertising and promotional campaign for your target customers. You must consider the following:

♦ What message do I want to convey to my prospects and customers?

♦ What type of advertising media is most appropriate for my business?

♦ How much can I afford to spend on my advertising?

Prior to answering these questions, it is important to remember that your advertising should be directed at your target market and that it must be continuous to be effective. If you have adequately identified your target market, then you should have little difficulty reaching your prospects using cost-effective media. Consider a software vendor that sells accounting and productivity applications to manufacturing businesses. Appropriate advertising media for this vendor might include direct mailings, trade shows, and listings in trade journals. Also, this vendor might visit the same two trade shows every year and conduct direct mailings to the same individuals every quarter.

Your publicity and promotion should gradually change the awareness level of prospective customers about your products and services. Remember your first day of school or college, when you didn't know anyone and said only a few brief hellos to your fellow classmates? At the end of the week, through multiple contacts, you knew some names and had even developed a few personal relationships. Finally, by the end of the school year you had developed full-blown friendships. Correctly implemented, your publicity and promotion will work the same way.

Imagine a new landscaping business that has targeted local office parks as its customers. Because the local building managers have never heard of this business and normally sign yearly contracts for service, the new landscaping business might try the following:

- Place an advertisement in the phone book under "landscaping."
- Call the local office parks and find out the names of the respective building managers.
- Begin mailing letters and fliers to the building managers every four to six weeks.
- After the fourth mailing, follow up with a phone call to see if the building managers are interested in learning more about the service.

Location

Location can lead to the success or ruin of your business. Because location requirements vary by the type of business, it is important to evaluate different selection criteria. For a merchandising business, choosing the right location usually involves trade-offs between customer convenience and the rent expense. For a manufacturer or wholesaler, access to public transportation, such as planes, trains, and interstate highways, is much more important.

As a retailer, you might ask yourself, "Where are my potential customers relative to my store location?" Consider why there is such a difference in rent expense between Beverly Hills in California and the small college town of Athens in Georgia. In Beverly Hills, on streets such as Rodeo Drive, thousands of potential customers with money to spend walk in front of the retail stores every day. Many of the retailers do not even have to advertise, there are so many customers with money to spend. In Athens, however, there is mainly a student population with little or no disposable income, and the retailers must constantly find ways to entice the students to spend their money. As you search for a retail location, it is important to remember that your rent expense includes not only the cost of space but also the amount of publicity and promotion you will have to conduct.

If you are a manufacturer or wholesaler, your location needs are entirely different than a retailer. You do not need direct access to the final purchasers of your products and services, you only need access to the distribution systems, like the railways and airports. Low-cost space becomes important to your profitability. Additionally, you might want to be near an area that has plenty of skilled workers in your line of business. If you are building jet airplanes, there will have to be some "rocket scientists" in the vicinity.

Depending on your line of business, some questions that will need to be answered in your business plan include:

- What is the address of your business?
- If your business is merchandising or retailing what are the consumer traffic patterns? How many people walk by your store every day?
- If your business is manufacturing or wholesaling, where is the closest airport? Interstate highway? Railway line?

- ◆ Are there other similar businesses near this location?
- ◆ How many square feet will your business occupy?
- ◆ What size vehicles have access to the loading dock?
- ◆ Will you lease or own the space?
- ◆ How much will remodeling and upgrades cost?
- ◆ Are there any zoning restrictions in the area?
- ◆ What benefits does this location offer your customers? What benefits does it offer your business?

Distribution channels

Unless you are starting a retail business, where all of your sales will be through a storefront, you will have to select the most appropriate channel(s) of distribution for your business. Channels of distribution get your products and services to the end customer. If you are a manufacturer, your products may flow through a wholesaler, and then to a retailer, before getting to the end customer.

To give you an idea about the variety of distribution channels, think of the ways you can buy a CD today. They include music clubs, retail stores, television home shopping channels, Internet stores, and mail-order catalogs.

All of the ways you can purchase a CD represent different channels of distribution for the manufacturer of CDs.

You must use channels of distribution that let customers buy your products and services when and where they want to buy them. If your customers want to buy things over the Internet, through retail stores, or with mail-order catalogs, then you must give them that opportunity. If your store is only open from 10 a.m. to 5 p.m. on weekdays, then you are effectively closing down your channel of distribution for some percentage of your market that is at work during these hours.

If you don't provide all of the channels of distribution that your customers want, then they will find a competitor to satisfy their needs. Think about mail order catalogs or the Internet—channels that are open 24 hours per day, seven days per week. These mediums give customers the opportunity to buy products and services all day and all night, and fully satisfy the "when" requirement. However, not everyone wants to buy clothes, books, or music through catalogs or over the Internet (they want to try them first). Therefore, these channels don't meet the "where" requirement. You must mix and match your channels to provide a "where" and "when" for a large percentage of your target market.

Marketing budget and timeline

Your marketing plan must account for the amount of money your are going to spend on advertising, publicity, and promotion. Additionally, you should develop a timeline for when you are planning to spend it. Although trade figures for established businesses might indicate advertising expenditures that are 5 percent of total sales, you will be much wiser to itemize the expenditures in a "bottoms-up" approach. This is especially important for a new business, rather than for an established business whose name and products are already known.

The "bottoms-up" approach to developing a budget recognizes the individual advertising and promotion activities that your business will perform throughout the year. For instance, a startup business might plan to place an advertisement in the phone book, run promotions through local newspapers, perform targeted direct mailings, and conduct face-to-face sales calls. The budget for these activities could be broken down as follows:

	Jan.	Feb.	Mar.	Apr.	May	June
Phone book	General ad $89/mo	General ad $89/mo	General ad $89/mo	General ad $89/mo	General ad $89/mo	General ad $89/mo
Local paper	Grand opening $150/wk			5-15% discount $150/wk		
Direct mail	Top 1,000 prospects $600/shot		Top 1,000 prospects $600/shot		Top 1,000 prospects $600/shot	
Sales calls		2 per day $200/visit	2 per day $200/visit	2 per day $200/visit	2 per day $200/visit	2 per day $200/visit

Your advertising budget will implicitly incorporate the sales goals for your business. If you need to sell 100 units of product per month to reach your end-of-year total sales goal of 1,200 units, then you must estimate the amount of advertising and selling effort that will be required to sell each unit. This is difficult for new businesses because they don't have any history; however, a little common sense can help. To sell 100 units every month means that on average you need to sell five units every day (using a 20 workday month). If one in 10 (10 percent) of your prospective customers makes a purchase, then you will have to interest 50 customers in what you have to sell every day.

It is important to remember that your advertising and promotion must be continuous, because there will be little direct correlation between a particular sale and your advertising. You cannot just start advertising to offset a decrease in sales, and stop advertising to maintain your profits. If you have identified your target market and selected the most appropriate media to reach your prospects, then developing a budget to meet your sales goals will be straightforward.

Chapter 9

Management and Personnel

Questions to be answered in this chapter:

- Why are you and your management team going to be successful?
- What previous experience do you have in this business?
- Are you lacking any managerial skills? How are you going to get these skills?
- What type of organizational structure does your business have?
- What are the responsibilities of each member of the management team?
- How many people work for your business? Are you going to hire more?
- How do you recruit and train employees?

Have you ever seen a coach explaining a game plan or mapping out a strategy during a competitive sporting event. Envision the coach standing in front of the team, chalk in hand, and a series of X's and O's on the blackboard. For your business plan, you are the coach and captain of the team, explaining to investors or management on the sidelines how your players are going to win the game. Not only must you explain how you will win, but you must also tell why this group of players has the skills necessary to beat the competition.

The management section of your plan describes the capabilities and talent that your team brings to the table to execute your business strategies. If you cannot document that your team has the management skills necessary to be competitive in the marketplace, investors will be unlikely to put any money into your business. Further, if you believe that you can do it all with little or no support in the key areas of marketing, operations, finance, and human resources, then you will be in for a big surprise after you open your doors for business. The competition will crush you, in order to take advantage of any opportunity that you identified in your business plan and are bringing to market.

Your management team is responsible for the operational and financial performance of your company. Through their direction, your employees will perform well or poorly. To eliminate as much risk as possible for poor performance, ensure that your management team has the experience and incentive necessary to motivate its employees.

One way that you and your team can influence the work environment at your company is through the organizational structure. The structure is important because it can often determine how successfully products are brought to market and managed through their life cycle. Your organizational chart displays functional responsibilities and the chain of command. Problems that occur lower in the organization may eventually move up and become your responsibility to resolve.

Description of the management team

This section of your plan explains how your team, yourself included, will be able to run the business successfully by identifying the responsibilities, strengths, and weaknesses of your key players. You will have to explain how you are going to fill any skill deficiencies and correct apparent team weaknesses. For skill deficiencies, you will either have to get the experience yourself or hire someone from outside the company.

Assume that you have developed a new product and want to bring it to market. If your skills are grounded in research and development or technical operations, then you will need to hire a sales professional to sell your product. It is not realistic for you to assume that after many years in the lab, you can turn yourself into a great salesperson. On the other hand, if you were born to sell, then you will need to obtain financing and operational skills from other individuals.

Investors will want to know about your background and that of the management team in detail. Questions that you must answer include:

♦ How long have you been with the company?
♦ What is your work experience?
♦ What companies have you worked for in the past?
♦ What were your responsibilities?
♦ What professional titles did you hold?
♦ How many people did you manage and in what capacity?
♦ What work and education experiences are transferable to your new position?
♦ How old are you?
♦ Where do you live?
♦ Are you a member or director of any organizations in your community?

Following is an example description of the management team for South Mill, Inc. Notice that this section starts with the name, age, and title of each management team member, and then follows with a more complete description of these individuals. Also, note that South Mill highlights a skill deficiency in its management team by explaining in detail that it has not hired a chief financial officer.

A sample description of management

The names, ages, positions, and business experience of South Mill's management team are provided below:

Name	Age	Position
Howard T. McBain	42	President and Chief Executive Officer
Sally Grant	48	Vice President of Sales and Marketing
Robert F. Levitt	45	Vice President of Operations
Nancy B. Dalton	51	Vice President of Human Resources and Personnel
Timothy H. Brooks	31	Controller

Howard T. McBain founded South Mill in 1986 and subsequently became the president and chief executive officer after the company was incorporated in 1987. Prior to starting South Mill, Mr. McBain was employed by the Fruit of the Loom company from 1980 to 1986 in a variety of manufacturing positions—most recently as plant manager in Charleston, South Carolina. Mr. McBain received a B.S. in industrial engineering from California Institute of Technology.

Sally Grant has been vice president of sales and marketing since October 1996. She served as the director of sales and marketing for wholesale and large retail customers from February 1992 to October 1996 and as an account manager for some of South Mill's major customers from March 1988 to February 1992. Prior to joining the company in March 1988, Ms. Grant worked as a buyer for two local retailers. Ms. Grant received a B.A. in humanities from the University of Georgia.

Robert T. Levitt has been vice president of operations since the company was incorporated in 1987. Prior to joining the company, Mr. Levitt was employed by the Fruit of the Loom company from 1975 to 1987, where he held various positions in manufacturing and labor relations. His last assignment was as the chief labor negotiator for the company. Mr. Levitt holds a B.S. in manufacturing technology from the University of Florida.

Nancy B. Dalton has been vice president of human resources and personnel since March of 1991 and as director of personnel since April of 1989. Prior to joining the company, she was a self-employed benefits consultant from August 1980 to April 1989. From May 1964 to August 1980, Ms. Dalton was a homemaker. Ms. Dalton received a certificate of personnel administration from DeKalb Community College.

Timothy H. Brooks has been controller since joining South Mill in July 1996. Mr. Brooks has more than seven years of experience in both public accounting and private industry. From January 1990 until July 1996, he was employed by Arthur Andersen as an auditor. Mr. Brooks received a B.S. in accounting from the University of Georgia and has passed the Uniform Certified Public Accounting exam.

To date, South Mill has not found it necessary to hire a full-time chief financial officer and has instead relied on Howard T. McBain, its president and chief executive officer, and the accounting firm of Arthur Andersen to manage the company's finances. In July 1996, South Mill hired Timothy H. Brooks to be its controller, but Mr. Brooks has had only limited involvement with the information presented in this plan. By the middle of 1998, South Mill intends to start a search for a chief financial officer.

Functional responsibilities

Because the management team is critical to the success of your business, you must document its ability to lead, plan, organize, and control. From your work experience, participation in team sports, or other group activities, you will recall that everyone has certain responsibilities according to his or her function. In the workplace, some people make the products, while others collect the money and pay the bills. On a sports team, there are offensive players responsible for scoring and defensive players who have to keep the other team from scoring. The winning team is usually led by a strong captain, has good players, and is well-organized.

Start by identifying the types of functions that will be required by your business. For illustrative purposes, assume that your management team will be made up of five individuals including yourself. The major functions of marketing, finance, operations, and personnel could then be assigned as in the chart on page 71.

Each of these functions must be assigned to someone on your team. If there are only two of you initially, then you might divide the major functions evenly based on your skill sets. Gaps will have to be filled by consultants or contractors.

Organization structure

Once your business grows beyond a few employees, you will no longer have the opportunity to interact with all of your customers and suppliers. This work will gradually be parceled out to your management team, and then to your employees. How your employees handle these "front-line" relationships will be based largely on the work environment and incentives that you establish.

Key factors to consider when you design your organization structure are:

♦ What type of organization structure do you have (functional, division, matrix, or other)?

- ◆ How many managerial levels are between you and your customers? Your suppliers?
- ◆ What measurement system do you use to measure employee performance?
- ◆ Do you have an employee survey to measure attitudes and job satisfaction?

Your organization structure will establish reporting relationships within your company and outline the roles and responsibilities for all employees. The following are some typical organization structures.

Functional responsibility	Your-self	Individual #1	Individual #2	Individual #3	Individual #4
Marketing					
• Sales		x			
• Product management		x			
• Advertising		x			
• Pricing		x			
• Packaging		x			
• Distribution		x			
Finance					
• Controller	x				
• Accounts receivable			x		
• Accounts payable			x		
• Inventory control			x		
• Billing			x		
• Treasury	x				
• Budgeting	x				
Operations					
• Inventory control			x		
• Location management				x	
• Purchasing			x		
• Production			x		
• Receiving				x	
Personnel					
• Recruiting	x				
• Training					x
• Benefits					x
• Compensation					x

Functional organization

The functional structure organizes all employees around typical business functions, such as marketing, operations, finance, and human resources. For instance, in a manufacturing business, employees responsible for making the products would report to one manager, while employees responsible for selling and distributing the products would report to a different manager.

This structure is very efficient when the type and variety of products being sold is limited. For instance, a manufacturing business with a single product line would use the functional organization structure. Because everyone always does the same tasks, they become very skilled in their jobs, and the organization becomes very efficient.

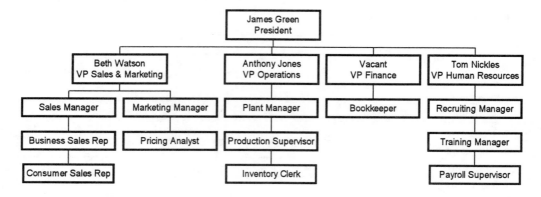

Unfortunately, as the business expands with more product lines, this structure becomes too confining. Different product lines often require different production skills and different channels of distribution. Take the auto manufacturer that produces everything from economy cars to diesel engines for large trucks. It would not be effective to have the same salespeople selling both the economy cars and the diesel engines, because the target audiences are significantly different. In this case, the division organization would be more appropriate.

Division organization

Once your company expands beyond the single product or product line, you should consider organizing by division. Essentially, this organization structure is like having multiple functional organizations within the same company. Divisions can be made responsible for a product, target market, or geographic area. For instance, an auto manufacturer might set up one division to sell economy cars and one to sell diesel engines. Both of these divisions would have separate factories, production workers, and salespeople. They might share common personnel and payroll functions, however.

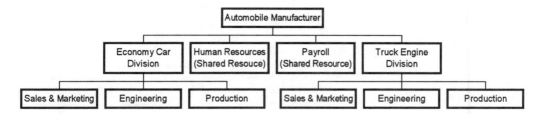

The advantage of the divisional structure, for a multiproduct-line company, is that individual focus can be given to separate product lines. It is almost like having a lot of smaller companies contained in one large company. Unfortunately, this structure can lead to internal conflicts as the different divisions compete for the same resources. It is also less efficient than the functional structure, because there is a duplication of resources. You need to have two sales groups, two engineering groups, and two production groups, each with their own management structure.

Matrix organization

The matrix organization attempts to combine the effectiveness of the divisional organization with the efficiency of the functional organization. In the matrix organization, functional employees are brought together in teams to work on special projects until they are complete. In this case, employees have two bosses for every project: their functional manager and a team leader for the special project.

The advantage of a matrix organization is that it provides flexibility for your company to complete special projects. Some of your best people from every department can be put together on a team to bring a new product to market quickly. People can also work on multiple projects at the same time, depending on resource limitations.

Although this type of organization provides more flexibility than the other two, it can cause a great deal of strain on the individual team members because of the reporting relationships. When you have employees reporting to a functional manager and a project manager at the same time, conflicts will occur. This week's priority for the functional manager may be entirely different than this week's priority for the project manager.

Management salaries

It is important for you to document the salaries, bonuses, and stock options for your management team. Salary treatment should not be too extravagant, as the payoff will come later on after the business is a success. Neither should it be too paltry, because investors will not believe you. As supporting documentation, you should include a salary history for each member of your management team.

Matrix Organization

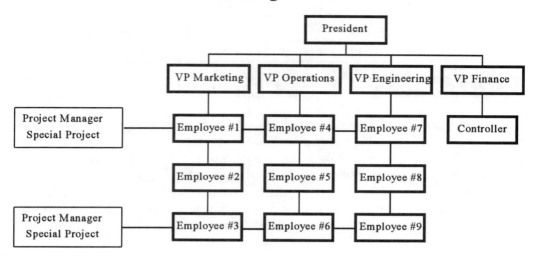

If you are applying for a loan or looking for venture capital, investors will want to know how much of your own money is at risk. The thought process is that you will be extremely motivated to make this business a success if you have a lot to lose. On the other hand, if you are not taking much of a financial risk, investors might feel that you might give up on their investment at the first sign of trouble.

For yourself, you should prepare a set of personal financial statements that show your income requirements to cover your living expenses and a statement of net worth. Examples of these documents are provided here:

Personal net worth statement

	Total amount	Comments
Assets		
• Home	$	
• Contents of home	$	
• Cars	$	
• Savings plan 401(K):	$	
• Bank accounts	$	
Total assets	$	
Liabilities		
• Mortgage	$	
• Credit card balances	$	
• Car loans	$	
• School loans	$	
• Other loan balances	$	
Total liabilities	$	
Personal net worth	$	Subtract total liabilities from total assets

Personal income requirement (per month)

Monthly expenses	Avg.	Comments
Household		
• Mortgage or rent expense (include taxes, insurance, and maintenance)	$	Variable rate mortgage that will increase/decrease
• Electricity	$	Increase in summer for AC
• Gas	$	Increase in winter for heating
• Phone	$	
• Water	$	
• Cable television	$	
Automobile		
• Car payment	$	Payments will cease next year
• Insurance	$	
• Gasoline	$	
• Maintenance	$	
Food		
• Grocery store	$	
• Restaurants	$	
• Cafeteria	$	
Education		
• College	$	Monthly savings
• After school programs	$	
Credit cards		
• Visa/MC/American Express	$	
• Department store	$	Pay off next month
Other		
• Magazine/newspaper subscriptions	$	
• Health club	$	
• Medical prescription	$	
• Charity	$	
• Estimated tax payments	$	
• Vacation	$	
• Clothes and laundry	$	
TOTAL	$	

Outside resources

In addition to your organization chart, you will have to rely on some outside resources for your business. Normally, these would include a lawyer, banker, accountant, and insurance broker. List them in your plan, including names and addresses, and the support that they will provide. For instance, if your accountant will prepare a set of yearly financial statements or if your lawyer will help you to incorporate, list these duties in your business plan.

There are many other resources that you can use to run your business. Companies that need help with hiring often engage the services of a recruiting firm or consultant. Computer businesses tend to hire contractors to help them with large programming projects. Manufacturers can engage part-time workers to help with spikes in production. College and university students can be used to conduct market research. Be creative in developing your resource plan, and recognize that all of the functions must be performed to some degree, and if you can't identify someone else to do the work, then you will be doing it yourself.

Personnel

This part of the management plan identifies everyone below the management team. Unless you are starting a professional services firm, these individuals will determine the strength or weakness of your organization. In this section you will have to identify how you are going to recruit, select, train, and pay your employees. For a business that is just beginning, recruiting and selection of good people is critical to the success of the business.

Provide answers to the following questions about the employees you are planning to hire:

♦ How many people do you need to hire "just to get the first product or service out of the door?"

♦ How many employees will you need to get to full production?

♦ Are the skills you need readily available in your market?

♦ If not, how much training will you need to educate your work force?

♦ How much will you pay part-time employees? Full-time employees?

♦ Describe your benefits package, including medical insurance, paid vacation, company holidays, and 401(K) plan.

Look at the sample description of personnel for Sales Training Group. Note that the company identifies the number of employees by function and the skills that they need to have. It also explains the training that its own employees must undergo, and briefly touches on the salary and benefits offered by the company.

A sample description of personnel

By December 31, 1997, Sales Training Group had 15 full-time employees, six of which were training professionals, three of which were sales representatives, and three of which were administrative staff. Sales Training Group believes that its continued success depends on recruiting, retaining, and motivating professionals at all levels in the company. Sales Training Group seeks to hire personnel with prior training or sales experience, with strong project management and communications skills. Most recruiting is conducted by an outside firm, with final hiring decisions made by the management team.

Sales Training Group provides training for new and existing employees to ensure that they are familiar with the latest trends in technology and are able to communicate clearly at all levels in a client's organization. Training covers computer and hardware topics that are relevant to a direct selling organization, presentation skills, and project and time management skills.

Sales Training Group attracts and motivates its employees by offering competitive compensation and benefit packages. All professionals are eligible for performance-based bonuses and yearly salary reviews. Sales Training Group has been able to retain 75 percent of its employees for the past three years.

In summary, the "Management and Personnel" section of your business plan identifies who you will be working with to make your business a success. For yourself and other key members of your team, investors will want to see some detail on your respective backgrounds and how you plan to organize. They will want to know who is in charge of sales, who is going to head up production, and who is responsible for paying the bills. These investors will also want to know how many people you are planning to employ and how much you are going to pay them, because payroll is usually the largest business expense.

Chapter 10

Finances

Questions to be answered in this chapter:

 ♦ Is your business profitable? If not, when will it be profitable?
 ♦ How fast will your sales and profits grow in the next three years?
 ♦ What is your business worth?
 ♦ Does your business have positive or negative cash flow?
 ♦ What is your breakeven point?

Do you balance your own checkbook every month? To the penny? Your answers to these questions say a lot about how you will approach the financial management section of your business plan. If you do balance your checkbook, then you already understand the importance of maintaining your personal finances, and it is simply a matter of transferring these skills to your business plan. If you don't balance your checkbook, but your spouse or accountant does, then you will probably have to get some assistance for this section of your business plan. If your checkbook is never balanced, then you may want to reconsider going into business and try the lottery instead!

Financial management tells you how much money you are making, how you are spending it, how much you have left over, and whether you need to change your spending habits to stay out of trouble. By planning ahead, you'll know whether you have enough money to take on new projects, or if you will need additional financing from investors or banks. As you plan your business, keep in mind that you will need money for capital investment (machines, equipment, and buildings), business expenses (salaries, supplies, and inventory), and most importantly, for you and your family.

The key to successful financial management is your accounting system. It will help you to monitor your sales, control your expenses, and realize your profitability objectives. You'll need to have a bookkeeping system that gives you enough information to prepare the following key documents:

 ♦ Balance sheet
 ♦ Income statement
 ♦ Cash flow statement

These three documents, along with a few financial ratios, act much like the dials and gauges on the dashboard of your car. They tell you if your business has enough gas, whether it is about to overheat, how far you have traveled (and how far you have to go), and when you need professional help to fix a problem. You must keep your eyes on the road and pay attention to early warning signals to stay out of trouble.

If you are not comfortable with numbers and accounting systems, you can do some of the following to improve your financial management plan:

- ♦ Go to the library or bookstore and get some reference books on accounting.
- ♦ Take a class at your local community college.
- ♦ Seek the help of an accountant or finance professional.

Balance sheet

Much like your personal net worth statement, a balance sheet shows what your business owns (assets), what its debts are (liabilities), and the difference between the two (equity). Think of a balance sheet this way: If the only thing you owned was a car with a value of $8,000, and you had taken out a $6,000 bank loan to finance the car, then your personal balance sheet would show an asset of $8,000, a liability of $6,000, and equity of $2,000. In real life you probably own many things—a house, a car, and a variety of personal items—and have numerous debts, such as a mortgage, a car loan, and credit card balances.

Similarly, in business you will have a few assets, such as cash and equipment, and a few liabilities, such as accounts payable and bank loans. These are shown on your balance sheet, which tells you what your business would be worth if you sold all of your assets and paid off all of your liabilities.

The balance sheet for your company will be divided into three parts and will conform with the following formula:

$$\text{Assets} = \text{Liabilities} + \text{Owner's Equity}$$

All balance sheets, whether for General Motors or Paul's Pizza Shop, have the same general format. Assets go at the top of the page, liabilities in the middle, and owner's equity at the bottom. Alternatively, assets can be listed on the left-hand side of the page, and liabilities and owner's equity on the right.

Assets, such as cash, inventories, and buildings, are always listed in decreasing order of liquidity. This means that cash and equivalents are always listed first, and the things that are hardest to convert to cash, such as buildings and equipment, are listed last. Liabilities are shown according to their immediacy of payment. For instance, bills that are due right away, such as payroll, come first, and debts that will not be paid off for years in the future come last.

The main distinction between balance sheets from different companies is the amount of detail they provide. Because General Motors is a large company, its balance sheet must provide significantly more detail than that of Paul's Pizza Shop. Greater detail is usually required to meet the information needs of a much wider audience, including investors, bankers, and management. Your balance sheet should be designed to provide enough detail to make it useful for you to manage your business and to meet the information requirements of your investors and bankers. No more, no less.

The example balance sheet for South Mill, Inc., has most of the items that you will want to display on the balance sheet for your company. Also, note that it is dated for the year ending December 31, 1998. By their nature, balance sheets show assets, liabilities, and owner's equity at a specific point in time. Normally this is the last day of your accounting, or fiscal, year.

South Mill, Inc.
Balance sheet: December 31, 1997

Assets	Amount	Description
Current assets	$1,207,860	Cash or other assets that will be converted to cash during the year, including marketable securities, receivables, prepaid expenses, and inventories.
Long-term investments	$450,000	Investments that are to be held for many years, such as stocks and bonds.
Property, plant, and equipment, less accumulated depreciation	$1,561,590	Physical property that is long-lasting and used in the regular course of business, such as land, buildings, machines, furniture, and office equipment.
Other assets	$349,270	Restricted to intangibles such as copyrights and patents.
Total assets	$3,568,720	Sum of all of the assets listed above.
Liabilities and owner's equity		
Current liabilities	$785,000	Obligations that are expected to be paid off in the current year, including: accounts payable, wages and taxes owed, and any long term debt that is due this year.
Long-term debt	$1,776,800	Debts that are to be paid off after the current year, such as mortgages and bank loans. Any payments for the current year should be shown in current liabilities.
Total liabilities	$2,561,800	Sum of all of the liabilities listed above.
Owner's equity or net worth	$1,006,920	Shown here as simply assets minus liabilities. Public companies often show additional categories of capital stock and retained earnings.
Total liabilities and owner's equity	$3,568,720	Sum of total liabilities and owner's equity.

If you are starting a new business, you may want to prepare a balance sheet to show where your business is today, where it will be at the end of the year, and where it will be at end of the following year.

Income statement

To understand how much money your business will make during the year, you will prepare an income statement, also referred to as a profit and loss (P&L) statement. While your balance sheet tells you how much money you have (owner's equity), an income statement tells you how much money you made (net income). You start by showing your sales revenue at the top of the statement, followed by your costs and expenses in the middle, and the difference, or net income, at the bottom.

Net income, or profit, is determined by subtracting all of your expenses from sales revenue, as shown in the following formula:

Sales Revenue - Expenses = Net Income (or Profit)

The income statement is also directly tied to your balance sheet. If you were operating a profitable business and prepared a set of financial statements at the end of the year, your owner's equity and assets would increase by the amount of net income shown at the bottom of the income statement— much like your bank account increases after you make a deposit. Conversely, if you had a loss, your owner's equity and assets would decrease by this amount.

Your income statement records the sales, expenses, and net profit for your business during a specific period of time. It could be for a week, a month, a quarter, a year, or whatever accounting cycle is important for your business. By looking at series of income statements, say for three consecutive years, you can get a good idea of where the business is headed from the trend in sales, expenses, and profits.

For your business plan, you will be most interested in *pro forma* or projected income statements. Projected financial statements are created to show how you think your business will perform financially in the future. They take into account your past financial performance (if you have any), along with assumptions about the future of your products and services, your target market, and your industry.

Normally, you will want to create pro forma income statements for the next one to three years. For most businesses, it should not be necessary to go more than three years, because the further out the projections, the more inaccurate they will be.

South Mill, Inc.
Pro Forma Income Statement
For the Year Ended December 31, 1998

	Amount	Description
Net sales revenue	$6,486,865	Total sales, less discounts, returns, and allowances. If you have revenue not related to the sales of products or services, such as rental revenue, add a line called "Other revenue."
Cost of goods sold	$5,068,188	Cost of inventory, including delivery-in, that has been sold.
Gross profit	$1,418,677	Net sales revenue minus cost of goods sold.
Expenses		
Sales and administrative	$413,370	Wages and salaries, travel, advertising, shipping, postage, office supplies, utilities, telephone, professional fees, and insurance.
Depreciation	$227,040	Current portion of depreciation for fixed assets, such as machinery and owned buildings.
Interest on long-term debt	$142,100	Includes interest on bonds and notes.
Other expense	$36,250	
Total expenses	$818,760	Sum of all expenses.
Income (loss) before taxes	$599,917	Gross profit less total expenses.
Taxes	$227,040	Federal and state taxes.
Net income (loss)	$372,877	Income before taxes minus taxes.

Sales forecast

To create your pro forma income statement, start at the top with your anticipated sales revenue or sales forecast. This is probably the most important number that you will try to predict, so take your time and do the research. One way to start is by looking at similar businesses in your industry.

For similar businesses, determine the following:

♦ What is their annual sales revenue?

♦ What is their annual unit volume?

♦ What is their average selling price?

You should already have most of this information in the marketing section of your business plan. If you have categories or classes of products and services, break the information down to give it as much meaning as possible.

	Product A	Product B	Product C	Total
Unit volume	500	200	800	1,500
Average price	$10	$30	$5	$10
Sales revenue	$5,000	$6,000	$4,000	$15,000

If possible, check your forecast to see if it makes sense. Compare it to your market using the following formula:

$$\text{Sales Revenue (or Customers)} = \text{Total Market Size} * \text{Market Growth Rate} * \text{Your Market Share}$$

- ◆ Total market size is an estimate of potential sales revenue for the entire market or industry. You should develop estimates from your past experience, market research, industry publications, and trade associations.
- ◆ Market growth rate is a percentage estimate of how fast the overall market or industry is growing. If you cannot find anything for the growth of your market niche, use the overall industry growth rate for this variable.
- ◆ Market share is your percentage estimate of how much sales revenue you are going to capture in the total market. This will be based on your marketing plan and take into account the strength of the competition, your product and service benefits, and financial resources.

Estimating expenses

In addition to creating a sales forecast for your pro forma income statements, you will also need to estimate the associated expenses. Start by breaking the expenses down as shown on the example income statement: cost of goods sold, sales and administrative expenses, depreciation, interest on long-term debts, other expenses, and taxes. There are two approaches you should take to estimating these expenses: a comparison with other companies in your industry and direct estimation.

Look at other companies in your industry with similar products and services. For instance, if you were planning to start a disk drive manufacturing business, you might want to look at the financial statements of Iomega Corporation. Iomega produces the Zip drive for personal computers and provides the financial statements online in its annual report.

As shown in the following chart, all of the expense items for Iomega can be expressed as a percentage of sales. For instance, you can calculate that Iomega's selling, general, and administrative (SG&A) expenses are 16.78 percent of sales, or $291,930 divided by $1,739,972. This percentage for SG&A expenses can then be applied to your sales revenue (forecasted earlier), to come up with an equivalent number for your business. Suppose that your sales forecast was for $1 million in revenue next year. Using the Iomega percentage of 16.78 percent, you would estimate that SG&A expenses for your business would be $167,779, or 0.1678 times $1 million.

Iomega Corporation and Subsidiaries
Consolidated Statements of Operations
For the year ended, December 31, 1997

	Iomega Results (in thousands)	Percent of Iomega Sales	Applied to Your Business
Sales	$1,739,972	100.00%	$1,000,000
Cost of sales	1,192,310	68.52%	685,247
Gross margin	547,662	31.48%	314,753
Operating expenses *:			
Selling, general, and administrative	291,930	16.78%	167,779
Research and development	78,026	4.48%	44,843
Total operating expenses	369,956	21.26%	212,622
Operating income	177,706	10.21%	102,132
Interest income	6,931	0.04%	3,983
Interest expense	(6,443)	(0.37%)	(3,703)
Other expense	(879)	(0.05%)	(505)
Income before income taxes	177,315	10.19%	101,907
Provision for income taxes	61,963	3.56%	35,611
Net income	115,352	6.63%	66,295

Source: http://www.iomega.com/company/investor/annualreport/about.html

*Note: Iomega does not break out depreciation expense in its consolidated expenses. However, if you look at the Consolidated Statements of Cash Flows, you will find it to be $39,272.

In a similar manner, you could estimate the other expenses for your business using the Iomega ratios. When you use this method to estimate expenses, keep the following key points in mind:

♦ Either use your own past results or pick businesses that are most similar to yours.

♦ Make allowances for life cycle. If you are just starting out, all of your expenses will be higher (relative to sales revenue) than a business that has been operating for a while.

♦ Adjust your estimates after you have been in business for six months to a year.

The direct approach to estimating expenses involves looking at each item individually and giving it a cost based on your forecasted volume. For instance, suppose you were starting a restaurant and were planning to serve 30,000 meals during the course of a year. Using this estimate for number of meals served, you could begin to estimate many of the items on the income statement, such as:

- ◆ GOGS = 30,000 * average meal cost (food + labor + service).

- ◆ Location expense = rent for space large enough to serve 100 meals per day (300 days per year).

- ◆ Depreciation = cost of equipment required to produce 30,000 meals ÷ 10 years.

- ◆ Interest expense = interest on loan for equipment to serve 30,000 meals.

Once you have developed estimates by looking at other companies in your industry and reviewing individual cost elements, compare the two estimates for a sense check. If there are large differences that you cannot explain, such as volume or pricing considerations, consider getting some outside advice from your accountant or industry trade association.

Cash flow statement

Keeping track of cash is one of the most important things that a new business can do. Without cash you can't buy inventory, pay salaries, or invest in equipment. It's entirely possible for a business to have assets on the balance sheet, to show a profit on the income statement, and still not have enough cash to keep going. This is analogous to the home owner who has paid off the mortgage, but doesn't have enough money to buy groceries. Plenty of assets, but no cash.

One reason for this phenomenon is the difference between cash basis accounting and accrual basis accounting. Cash basis accounting is intuitive, because you record sales when you receive money, and expenses when you pay bills. However, accrual accounting is less intuitive, because you record revenues when they are earned and expenses when they are incurred. For example, if you are using accrual accounting and provide credit to your customers, you may record sales revenue 90 days before you receive payment. Alternatively, think of an airline manufacturer that begins to recognize revenue on planes that won't be delivered for many years to come.

With accrual accounting, comes depreciation expense. Depreciation is a method used in accrual accounting to show how big-ticket items, such as machinery and equipment, lose value over time. In cash accounting, there is no depreciation, because the expense for the entire item is recorded when you pay the bill. In accrual accounting, on the other hand, depreciation might spread the expense over a period of years. For instance, a $25,000 machine might have $5,000 of depreciation expense over the next five years.

An example comparison of cash versus accrual basis accounting is shown in the following table:

	Cash basis	Accrual basis
Cash sales	$100,000	$100,000
Purchase equipment/depreciation	25,000	5,000
Income	75,000	95,000

Like the income statement, the cash flow statement is a summary of activity over time. You will show where your cash is coming from and what it is being used for. For instance, you will receive cash from customers when they make purchases and from banks when they give you a loan. You will use the cash to pay wages, buy inventory, and invest in property, plant, and equipment. In your business plan, you will want to produce a series of pro forma cash flow statements to cover at least the first 12 months after you start and the next two years.

At the top of your cash flow statement, start by listing where the cash is coming from, including sales of products and services, dividend and interest income, and financing from banks and investors. Keep in mind that you will make entries only for a given month or quarter, when you actually anticipate receiving the cash.

Next, itemize how you are planning to use the cash, including cost of goods sold, wages and salaries, rent, utilities, phone service, advertising, interest expense, equipment and machinery, and anything else that will require the transfer of cash out of your business. Although many of these entries may correspond to those that appear on your pro forma income statement, there should be differences. Timing differences between credit sales, cash received, and depreciation are two that were discussed earlier.

The difference between the cash coming into your business, and the cash going out, is called cash flow. A positive cash flow indicates that you have more cash coming into your business than going out. A negative cash flow means you have more cash going out of your business than coming in. Obviously, a business cannot withstand a negative cash flow for very long without running into trouble with creditors.

If you examine cash flow statements from some of the larger publicly traded companies in their annual reports, you will notice that the format is a combination of the income statement and the balance sheet. These companies prepare cash flow statements to show changes in balance sheet accounts and eliminate noncash items from income statements.

For instance, look at the following cash flow statement for South Mill. It starts by listing net income and then adds back to its noncash items such as depreciation.

Breakeven analysis

The breakeven point for your business is when it has zero income. That is when it is not making any money and it is not losing any money. Your breakeven point will occur when your level of sales is high enough to cover all

Finances

South Mill, Inc.
Statement of cash flows
For the period ended December 31, 1998

	1998	Description
Net income	$372,877	Start with net income
Adjustments to reconcile net income to net cash provided		
Provision for depreciation and amortization	227,040	Add back depreciation because it doesn't affect cash
Increase in accounts receivable	(198,612)	More sales on credit
(Increase) decrease in income taxes receivable	42,600	Received cash from income taxes
Increase in inventories	(337,685)	Cash used to make inventory
Increase (decrease) in accounts payable	100,000	Credit purchases
Increase in accrued expenses	64,416	Not paying bills
Increase (decrease) in note payable	(80,506)	Used cash to pay a loan
Net cash provided by (used in) operating activities	190,130	Sum of adjustments listed above
Cash flows from investing activities		
Purchases of property, plant, and equipment	(420,000)	Used cash to buy plant and equipment
Other, net	0	
Net cash used in investing activities	(420,000)	
Cash flow from financing activities		
Proceeds from issuance of long-term debt	500,000	Received a loan
Repayments of long-term debt	0	
Net borrowings from (repayments of) revolving loan	0	
Net cash provided by (used in) financing activities	500,000	
Net increase (decrease) in cash	270,130	Total cash flow for South Mill

of your variable and fixed costs. The formula for breakeven point can be expressed as,

Breakeven Sales Revenue = Fixed Costs + Variable Costs

Fixed costs do change with your sales level. From the day you start your business, you will have fixed costs that have no bearing on whether you sell millions of units or nothing at all. An example is rent expense. No matter what happens during the month in your retail store, the landlord will still want rent to be paid at the end of the month. The same goes for employees and bankers. These individuals do not care what your sales level was, they just want to be paid at the end of the month. Other examples of fixed expense include some portion of utilities and phone service, interest charges, employee benefits, and depreciation.

Variable costs change directly with your level of sales. Examples of variable costs include fabric used by clothing manufacturers, phone service used by telemarketers, tires used by automobile manufacturers, food used by restaurant owners, and commissions paid to salespeople.

Another way for you to calculate your breakeven point is to look at your average selling price and your unit variable costs, as follows:

$$\text{Breakeven Sales Units} =$$
$$\text{Fixed Costs} \div (\text{average selling price - unit variable cost})$$

Assume that you deliver newspapers and want to know how many you will have to deliver to break even. The cost of your bicycle is $200. You buy the papers for 20¢ each, and resell them for 25¢.

$$\text{Breakeven Sales Units} = 200 \div (.25 - .20)$$

This tells you that you will need to sell 4,000 newspapers to cover the cost of your bicycle, or to break even. After that point, your profit is 5¢ on every newspaper sold. Of course fixed costs could have also included insurance and maintenance, and the bike could have been depreciated for a few years.

Financing requirements

Many business plans are written for the purpose of obtaining a bank loan or seeking funds from outside investors. These plans must include a section on how these funds will be used and when they are required. For instance, you might write, "Next year our business will be expanding to support home deliveries and will require a vehicle estimated to cost $35,000." Make sure that you include lease agreements or purchase contracts for these planned expenditures.

Capital equipment list

Prepare a list of capital equipment for your business plan. Capital equipment is used in the production and delivery of your products and services, and might include delivery trucks, heavy machinery, computers, office furniture, phone systems, and permanent fixtures. Capital equipment normally lasts for many years and is depreciated over the course of its useful life.

Make sure your listing includes a description, date of purchase, and cost.

Financial ratios

By now you have devoted a considerable amount of time to your business plan and have created a full set of pro forma financial statements. Your last step is to compare these statements with similar businesses in your industry. You should do it now, because bankers, investors, and managers certainly will make these comparisons when you present them with your plan. This way you will be able to address their questions as they arise and avoid significant reworking of the plan. Getting it right now will save time later on when you really need it!

One of the best ways to compare your financial statements to those of other companies in your industry is by using ratio analysis. Ratios are a way of normalizing numbers, so that a comparison can be made to other businesses that may be significantly different in size. For example, if your nearest competitor has larger profits than your business, how can you say that your business is more profitable? If your ratio of profit to sales is higher than that of this competitor, then you can claim that your business is more profitable.

There are two main classes of ratios on which to base your comparison: profitability and liquidity. There are also a few other ratios that publicly traded companies use, such as the price-to-earnings (P/E) ratio and book value per share, that are not covered here.

Profitability ratios

Profitability ratios measure the overall success of your company. They compare your income with owner's equity, total assets, and sales revenue.

Return on equity (ROE) = net income (or net profit) ÷ owner's equity

The return on equity ratio shows the owners how well their investment has performed. Because income is what your business has left over after you have paid all of your expenses, interest, depreciation, and taxes, it can be divided by net income to calculate a return. This return (or percentage) must be higher than what an owner might earn with a much less-risky investment, such as earning interest in a bank account or even from a stock mutual fund.

Return on total investment (ROI) = net income ÷ total assets

Another measure of profitability is the ratio of net income to total assets. This ratio, normally called return on total investment, will always be less than return on equity, unless your business has no debt (remember that assets = liabilities + owner's equity). In that case the returns would be the same. This ratio gives you an idea of how well you are using all of the companies assets, including cash, investments, and property, plant, and equipment.

In some cases you may want to adjust the ROI ratio by adding interest expense to net income. This will have the effect of increasing the return, but also allows for the fact that your creditors have already received their returns through interest payments.

Net profit margin = net income ÷ net sales revenue

The net profit margin ratio is your net income (or profit) divided by your net sales revenue. A low net profit margin might mean that your costs and expenses are too high or your prices are too low. You can also calculate your gross margin on sales (gross profit ÷ net sales revenue) and your operating profit on sales (operating profit ÷ net sales revenue).

Liquidity ratios

Liquidity is a measure of how fast you can convert your assets to cash and pay off any bills that might come due in the near future. As with cash-flow analysis, bankers and investors want to see how much cash you have at your disposal.

Working capital = current assets ÷ current liabilities

The working capital ratio, or current ratio, is a measure of your company's liquidity. To calculate this ratio, use your balance sheet and divide current assets by current liabilities. Ratios that are close to 1.0 or less indicate trouble ahead, because you do not have enough cash or equivalents to pay off your current bills. Ratios that are 2.0 or more will not raise any red flags for bankers and investors. If your working capital ratio is between one 1.0 and 2.0, you may need some justification or seek additional working capital financing.

Quick ratio = quick assets ÷ current liabilities

The quick ratio is also a measure of liquidity. It is much "tougher," however, than the working capital ratio. This ratio excludes the value of inventory and prepaid expenses that were included in current assets of the working capital ratio. The reasoning is that sometimes it may be very difficult for you to convert inventory into cash in a timely manner. It would be difficult for the store owner to pay a bill in 30 days with inventory that won't be sold for 90 days or more.

Receivable turnover = net credit sales ÷ average trade receivables

Another ratio that says something about your liquidity is the receivable turnover ratio. This ratio describes how fast your business is able to collect cash for sales made on credit. Because terms tend to be 30, 60, or 90 days for payment, you would expect this ratio to be 12, 6, or 4, respectively. To convert your ratio to days, simply divide 360 days per year by your ratio. To calculate this ratio properly you will need to know the amount of sales your business makes on credit. Also you can use the accounts receivable from your balance sheet.

Inventory turnover = cost of goods sold ÷ inventory

Inventory turnover measures how quickly you sell your inventory. If you divide cost of goods sold by inventory on your balance sheet, you derive the average shelf life for your products. Inventory turnover depends very much on your industry. A grocery store may turn over its inventory every six days, with an inventory turnover ratio of 60, while an automobile dealer may turn over its inventory every 60 days, with an inventory turnover ratio of six.

Chapter 11

Sample Business Plan

This chapter contains a sample business plan for South Mill, a clothing manufacturer. South Mill has been in business for a number of years and now needs to expand its existing manufacturing facility to keep up with demand for its line of polo shirts and T-shirts. The company is seeking a $500,000 loan for its expansion plans.

As you write your business plan, it is important to remember that all plans differ in terms of strategy, format, content, and even in the type of language used. For instance, if you are starting a professional services business, such as an accounting or law firm, note that customers are referred to as clients and the actual work is called a client engagement. South Mill devotes a considerable portion of its plan to its manufacturing process, which would not be applicable to a professional services firm or a retailer. You must use the language of your industry and emphasize the key aspects of your business.

One of the best places to find business plan content that is relevant to the current environment is in the "S-1" documents filed by companies that are going through the Initial Public Offering (IPO) process with the Securities and Exchange Commission (SEC). Because these companies are trying to raise money from the public, they must pass a rigorous registration process with the government that involves describing their businesses, competitive environments, and strategies in detail. Best of all, these documents are available online through a couple of Web sites:

IPO Central

http://www.ipocentral.com

IPO Central describes itself as "the ultimate source of IPO information" and has a wealth of information on its Web site, including a search feature that allows you to find IPOs by company name, keyword, underwriter, state, or metro area. The list of companies you can find on this site goes back to May 6, 1996, the date after which companies were required to begin electronic filing with the SEC. Through this site, you can also get information from Hoover's Company Profiles and EDGAR Online.

EDGAR Online

http://www.edgar-online.com

As mentioned at the beginning of the book, the Internet puts information at your fingertips that previously could only be found in specialized libraries and government archives. Nowhere is this more true than the documents available from the SEC. Prior to EDGAR (Electronic Data Gathering Analysis and Retrieval), research on public companies had to be performed at the library on micro-fiche. Now using the Internet, you can access the latest documents filed with the SEC through EDGAR.

For your own plan, find companies at these Web sites that are as close to yours as possible. Don't be discouraged when you first look at the beginning of the "S-1" documents and see nothing but technical financial information. Find the Table of Contents and locate the pages that correspond with "Description of Business," "Industry Analysis," "Competition," etc.

BUSINESS PLAN

South Mill, Inc.

1234 West Main Street
Anywhere, Georgia 43112
(303) 555-1818

SIC 2335

October 20, 1997

Contact:
Howard T. McBain
President

Copy ___ of ____

Executive summary

South Mill is a vertically integrated manufacturer of high-quality polo shirts and T-shirts for men and women. The company plans to increase sales and profitability in the next three years by selling high-value products to wholesalers and retailers. The company expects to continue its sales growth of nearly 45 percent per year, to $13.6 million by the year 2000, while maintaining net profits at 8.5 percent of sales.

South Mill will meet its growth objectives by continuing to cost-effectively manufacture higher-quality polo shirts and T-shirts, and selling them to a wider variety of customers than other competitors in the industry. South Mill's continued expansion builds on its strategy to invest in the latest technology and utilization of flexible manufacturing methods.

Statement of purpose

South Mill seeks a total loan of $500,000 to expand its current manufacturing capacity at its plant in Anywhere, Georgia. The breakdown of this amount is as follows: $300,000 would be used to increase the size of its existing plant, including adding 7,000 square feet of floor space and upgrading electrical power for the entire building; $120,000 to purchase new knitting and dyeing machinery; and $80,000 to improve its working capital position. The expansion will help South Mill to reduce its current backlog of orders, increase total sales, and improve profitability.

Table of contents

Part I. The business

Part II. Financial data

Part III. Appendix (*)

(*) For brevity, these items have been excluded from the South Mill plan in this book. However, you may want to consider including some, or all, of these items in your plan.

Part I. The business

Description of business

South Mill sells its clothing to companies such as Ralph Lauren, Brooks Brothers, and Neiman Marcus. Additionally, the company sells its clothing using its own brand name to wholesale and retail customers such as Kmart and Sears. The company has increased net sales from $1.5 million in 1994 to $4.5 million in 1997, a compound annual growth rate of nearly 45 percent, and has been profitable since 1990.

South Mill was incorporated in November 1987 by certain members of the management team who collectively have more than 50 years of industry experience. Their vision was to cost-effectively manufacture higher-quality polo shirts and T-shirts and sell to a wider variety of customers than other competitors in the industry. To meet its objective of producing low-cost, high-quality clothing, South Mill invested in the latest technology available to manufacturers.

Since the business started, South Mill has been a leading manufacturer of polo shirts and T-shirts and has set new standards for styling and quality. The company was first to market with competitively priced clothing that used fiber-reactive dyes to reduce fading and rib-knit collars with more thickness to resist curling. Market acceptance of these products was rapid, and the company has been able to expand its sales and profitability every year by reaching more customer segments. In 1991, South Mill started manufacturing its line of polo shirts and T-shirts with long sleeves to diversify its product mix and use its production capacity more efficiently.

Additionally, South Mill works with customers to develop new products with unique styling. This gives the company a competitive advantage, because most of its competitors lack the flexible manufacturing facilities necessary to offer "made-to-order" services to their customers. That often leads the company to be chosen as the "manufacturer of choice" by large retailers and wholesalers.

Mission statement

South Mill will increase sales and profitability by providing high-quality polo shirts and T-shirts to an increasing number of customers. In order to accomplish this mission, South Mill has set the following goals and objectives:

- Producing high-quality apparel.
- Continued sales growth of 45 percent per year through greater channels of distribution.
- Expanding its existing product lines.
- Using state-of-the-art technology and machinery.
- Capitalizing on its flexible manufacturing methods.

Products

South Mill's polo shirts and T-shirts meet customer needs for high quality by providing rib-knit collars that resist curling, topstitching that looks sharp and adds strength, compacted fabric to resist shrinkage, and fiber-reactive dyes to prevent fading. The company's products are made of 100-percent cotton and can be purchased in a variety of styles, colors, and weights, with short or long sleeves. South Mill also provides custom embroidery services for customers to add company logos, emblems, trademarks, and service marks.

Relative to its competitors, South Mill's products are superior in design and quality for the following reasons:

- South Mill's polo shirts and T-shirts use 100-percent long-staple combed cotton for added softness.
- South Mill uses topstitching that provides a neater appearance and adds strength.
- South Mill's shirts contain 25 percent more tuck-stitches for added breathability in hotter temperatures.
- South Mill uses compacted fabric to resist shrinkage.
- South Mill colors its polo shirts and T-shirts with fiber-reactive dyes to prevent fading.

The sales mix and average selling price for men's and women's polo shirts and T-shirts for the years ended December 31, 1996 and 1997, is shown in the following table.

Years ending December 31	1997 Sales	1997 Units	1997 Avg	1996 Sales	1996 Units	1996 Avg
Men's						
• Woven sport shirts	$79,488	6,912	$11.50	$69,203	6,018	$11.50
• Knit T-shirts	$3,190,002	514,516	$6.20	$2,411,265	388,914	$6.20
Subtotal/Avg	$3,269,490	521,428	$6.27	$2,480,468	394,931	$6.28
Women's						
• Woven sport shirts	$356,432	44,805	$7.96	$227,125	29,219	$7.77
• Knit T-shirts	$847,778	186,973	$4.53	$487,907	93,139	$5.24
Subtotal/Avg	$1,204,210	231,778	$5.20	$715,032	122,358	$5.84
Grand total	$4,473,700	753,207	$5.94	$3,195,500	517,289	$6.18

Historically, South Mill's sales have been derived from T-shirts. However, the company introduced polo shirts in 1993 to diversify its product mix and increase the average selling price per unit sold. Also, the company was able to reduce the impact of seasonality after adding long sleeves to its product lines in 1994.

Industry and market analysis

South Mill competes in the growing market for casual dress clothes in the apparel industry. According to the Current Industrial Reports published by the U.S. Department of Commerce, industry shipments of polo shirts and T-shirts increased from $5.9 billion in 1995 to $6.3 billion in 1996, or by nearly 7 percent. For this same period, the value of shipments for men's polo shirts and T-shirts increased from $4.3 billion to $4.4 billion, or by 2 percent, while for women it increased from $1.5 billion to $1.9 billion, or by nearly 27 percent.

Description	1996 Units in Thousands	1996 Value in $Millions	1995 Units in Thousands	1995 Value in $Millions
Men's				
• Woven sport shirts	22,833	$255.1	24,769	$246.4
• Knit T-shirts	916,335	4,174.1	863,032	4,073.6
Subtotal	939,168	4,429.2	887,801	4,320.0
Women's				
• Woven sport shirts	102,386	814.5	81,292	631.9
• Knit T-shirts	243,526	1,104.2	174,630	914.8
Subtotal	345,912	1,918.7	255,922	1,546.7
Grand total	1,285,080	6,347.9	1,143,723	5,866.7

The growth of the polo shirts and T-shirt segments of the apparel industry can be attributed to several factors. First, the trends to become more physically fit and dressing more casually for work and social activities have made it acceptable for this type of clothing to be worn as daily attire. Second, the versatility of cotton fabric, in conjunction with advances in technology and manufacturing, have improved clothing design and quality, resulting in higher customer demand. Lastly, because the basic styles of polo shirts and T-shirts are not driven by fads or trends in fashion, consumer demand stays relatively stable.

As in most industries, consumers continually want more value for their money, including higher quality and greater variety at the same or lower prices. Consumers want polo and T-shirts that last longer, come in a variety of colors, and are comfortable enough to wear all day.

Recently, the channels of distribution to reach customers have become more diversified. In the past, polo shirts and T-shirts were distributed mainly through specialty clothing and department stores. Today, however, these articles of clothing can be purchased through mail order catalogs, mass merchandisers, the Internet, and other channels of distribution.

The growing number of distribution channels has given manufacturers the opportunity to serve more customers with a wider range of products. In order to meet these demands, manufacturers have had to adjust their business strategies to remain competitive. To address the consumer need for better quality at the same price, producers have upgraded their manufacturing processes by using newer technology and machinery. Additionally, to satisfy an increasing number of customers created by the new channels of distribution, manufacturers have had to become more flexible in their product development and production methods.

Customers

South Mill's market consists of four segments: name brand, wholesalers and large retail chains, value-added job shops, and specialty retailers. South Mill is able to meet the needs of this diverse set of customers because of its technology investments and flexible manufacturing processes. For the years ended December 31, 1997, 1996, and 1995, South Mill's top 10 customers accounted for 55 percent, 70 percent and 80 percent, respectively, of the company's total sales revenue.

Name-brand customers

South Mill's name-brand customers include Ralph Lauren, Brooks Brothers, and Neiman Marcus. South Mill produces polo shirts and T-shirts for these customers according to their specifications that include styling, size, color, logos, and trademarks. Pricing and contracts are negotiated yearly, based on the specifications and forecasted unit volumes. The shirts are labeled, packaged, and sent to the name-brand customers ready for sale to the end-consumer. Because of the "made-to-order" aspect of this segment, South Mill is usually able to extract price premiums and higher gross profit margins from these customers. Name-brand customers accounted for 50 percent of South Mill's revenue for the year ended December 31, 1997.

Wholesalers and large retail customers

South Mill's two largest retail customers in 1997 were Sears and Kmart. South Mill sells its polo shirts and T-shirts to these customers using its own brand name. These customers order from South Mill's standard catalog, by selecting sizes, colors, and styles at predetermined volume-discounted prices. The company has seen significant growth from this segment for the past three years, from 1995 to 1997, where sales have increased from 25 percent to 40 percent, respectively.

Value-added job shop customers

Value-added job shops purchase basic polo shirts and T-shirts from South Mill, and then add designs, logos, and trademarks, according to their customer specifications. For instance, a golf-pro shop may approach a value-added job shop and request a limited quantity of polo shirts with the embroidered name of the golf course. Although this segment was only 5 percent of South Mill's total sales in 1997, it helps the company to balance production by purchasing excess inventory.

Specialty retailers

South Mill's two largest specialty retail customers are Planet Hollywood and Warner Brothers.

For these retailers, with high name recognition and steady demand throughout the year from their retail outlets, South Mill provides the services normally associated with the value-added job shops. It sells these customers standard polo shirts and T-shirts that are either printed or embroidered with their logos or trademarks. The gains that South Mill has achieved in this segment in the past two years, has been partially at the expense of the value-added job shop segment. In 1997, company sales from this segment were 5 percent.

Seasonality

The market for polo shirts and T-shirts is seasonal. Normally, demand for short-sleeved shirts is much higher in the first and second quarters of the year, as retailers place orders for the spring and summer. Conversely, demand for long-sleeved polo shirts and T-shirts is higher in the third and fourth quarters, as retailers place orders for the fall and winter. However, this seasonality effect is also dependent on the geographic coverage of the retailer. Those with a predominantly southern customer base, with warmer climates year round, typically have a steady demand for only short-sleeved polo shirts and T-shirts. Retailers that are located in true four-season geographic areas are more likely to follow the seasonality trend described.

Marketing strategy

South Mill targets a wide variety of customers through multiple channels of distribution. Currently, South Mill's major customers include name-brand customers such as Ralph Lauren, Brooks Brothers, and Neiman Marcus, retailers such as Kmart and Sears, and specialty retailers such as Planet Hollywood and Warner Brothers. Additionally, South Mill sells to wholesalers and value-added job shops who, in turn, sell the company's polo shirts and T-shirts to numerous independent retailers, such as golf-pro shops and airport concession stands. South Mill plans to grow by retaining existing customers and acquiring new ones.

South Mill is recognized as a leading producer of high-quality polo shirt and T-shirt apparel at competitive prices by today's value-conscious consumers. Examples of South Mill's attention to quality can be found throughout its design and production processes. South Mill's polo and T-shirts meet customer needs by providing rib-knit collars that resist curling, topstitching that looks sharp and adds strength, compacted fabric to resist shrinkage, and fiber-reactive dyes to prevent fading.

South Mill creates new polo shirt and T-shirt designs to meet the exclusive requirements of its customers. The company usually receives a price premium for these new designs that results in a higher gross profit margin for each unit sold. Also, many new designs originally requested by one customer become popular with other customers as market acceptance increases. South Mill was first to introduce competitively priced fiber-reactive dyes to reduce fading and rib-knit collars with more thickness that resist curling.

Also, South Mill added long sleeves to both of its polo shirt and T-shirt product lines and received an increase in demand from customers who have a large base of consumers in colder climates.

South Mill markets to existing customers with its direct sales force. Sales managers are assigned according to one of the following customer segments: name brand, wholesalers and large retail chains, value-added job shops, and specialty retailers. Depending on the size and activity in each of these segments, the sales manager will in turn assign an account executive to single or multiple customer accounts within the segment. The sales team is responsible for responding to customer proposals, announcing special promotions, and communicating new developments about the company. South Mill also produces a quarterly newsletter that highlights any technology improvements, trends in the industry, and new customer acquisitions.

Members of South Mill's sales force participate in the sales incentive plan. Each year, South Mill establishes a level of annual sales volume for its target markets. At the end of the year, this established sales volume is subtracted from the company's actual sales results, and the difference is used to calculate the bonus for each market segment.

Competition

The market for polo shirts and T-shirts is very competitive. South Mill's major competitors are also vertically integrated manufacturers and include many larger businesses such as Sara Lee, Russell, and Fruit of the Loom, and smaller job-shop operations, including Truvalt West and True Shirt. In order to continue its success in this market, South Mill will maintain its focus on limited product lines (polo shirts and T-shirts) manufactured to the highest quality standards at competitive price points, and will use the most technologically advanced manufacturing processes and methods.

Manufacturing and operations

South Mill is a vertically integrated manufacturer that produces polo shirts and T-shirts with its own knitting, dyeing, finishing, cutting, sewing, and embroidery processes. By using the latest technology and machinery, in conjunction with flexible manufacturing methods, South Mill is able to optimize the production of its product lines. Although some of the company's competitors have moved production overseas, all of South Mill's products are manufactured at its plant in Anywhere, Georgia. This gives South Mill added flexibility to meet its customers' just-in-time delivery needs and reduces transportation costs.

South Mill is planning to expand its current manufacturing capacity at its plant in Anywhere, Georgia. The added capacity will help to reduce its current backlog of $1.2 million and increase sales by 40 percent to 50 percent per year. The planned capacity expansion includes increasing the size of its existing plant, adding 7,000 square feet of floor space, upgrading electrical power for the entire building, and purchasing new knitting and dyeing machinery.

South Mill's vertically integrated manufacturing process includes knitting, dyeing, finishing, cutting, sewing, and embroidering. Descriptions of each are as follows:

Knitting process

South Mill produces its own fabric using high-speed circular knitting machinery at its plant in Anywhere, Georgia. Circular knitting lowers a manufacturer's production costs by eliminating side-seaming and reducing waste. Because of its flexible manufacturing methods, South Mill is able to produce various types of cotton fabrics with minimal machinery downtime.

Dyeing process

South Mill colors its fabric using fiber-reactive dyes that reduce fading. Its state-of-the-art equipment gives the fabric colorfast hues by monitoring chemical usage, water temperature, and pressure. Additionally, computer controls help to speed up processing time and minimize waste.

Finishing process

After producing and coloring the fabric, South Mill dries, brushes, and compacts the fabric with its finishing process. South Mill has purchased the most technologically advanced brushing, or combing, machinery on the market to align the cotton fibers for maximum fabric softness.

Cutting process

All of South Mill's finished fabric is cut into shape with computer-controlled equipment that is linked to its pattern design process. Since introducing the fully automated cutting machinery into its manufacturing process in 1994, South Mill has been able to increase productivity by 25 percent and reduce waste by 15 percent.

Sewing process

The final stage of production is the sewing process. South Mill uses a combination of automated machinery and manual operators to assemble its polo shirts and T-shirts. Through this combination, South Mill is able to apply superior topstitching to its products for added strength and quality.

Embroidering process

When required, South Mill applies embroidery or screen printing to its polo shirts and T-shirts. Emblems and logos are applied by operators of the sewing and screen printing equipment.

Packaging and storage

Once South Mill's polo shirts and T-shirts have been assembled with its sewing process, or after they have been embroidered, they are ready to be packaged for distribution. Packaging includes applying tags to the shirts, folding them, placing them in plastic bags (when required), and bar coding. This entire process is automated using the latest packaging technology.

All of South Mill's packaged polo shirts and T-shirts are then stored in its warehouse located in Anywhere, Georgia. South Mill reduces the amount of inventory it has on hand by closely working with its customers' just-in-time systems. Its objective is to have all orders shipped within one week of final assembly. To monitor this objective, South Mill's finished goods are tracked throughout its warehouse with scanning technology and a centralized computer system.

Raw materials

South Mill buys yarn, dyes, and chemicals for its manufacturing process. Currently, there is no anticipated shortage of any of these raw materials, and they are priced competitively by suppliers. All raw materials are purchased under yearly contracts with local suppliers. In the event that one of these suppliers could not fulfill its obligations, South Mill believes that there are enough additional suppliers that could meet its raw material needs in the time required. South Mill keeps its raw materials inventory to a minimum, using the just-in-time capabilities of its management information system, and seeks to have no more than 10 day's supply on hand at any point in time.

Computer system and software

South Mill has installed the latest computer system and software to manage its entire business. All activity—from the time an order is placed by one of its customers, through its manufacturing process, until it leaves the shipping dock—is closely monitored by its management information system. In addition to tracking orders, this system facilitates South Mill's sales, distribution, and financial reporting requirements and helps it to manage the growth of its business.

Properties

South Mill's production facility and executive offices are housed in a 31,000-square-foot building located at 1234 West Main Street, Anywhere, Georgia. The company is currently seeking financing to expand its production facility by 7,000 square feet.

Management and organization

South Mill's management team, including its member's names, ages, positions and business experience, are provided below:

Name	Age	Position
Howard T. McBain	42	President and Chief Executive Officer
Sally Grant	48	Vice President of Sales and Marketing
Robert F. Levitt	45	Vice President of Operations
Nancy B. Dalton	51	Vice President of Human Resources and Personnel
Timothy H. Brooks	31	Controller

Howard T. McBain founded South Mill in 1986 and subsequently became the president and chief executive officer after the company was incorporated in 1987. Prior to starting South Mill, Mr. McBain was employed by the Fruit of the Loom company from 1980 to 1986 in a variety of manufacturing positions—most recently as plant manager in Charleston, South Carolina. Mr. McBain received a B.S. in industrial engineering from California Institute of Technology.

Sally Grant has been vice president of sales and marketing since October 1996. She served as the director of sales and marketing for wholesale and large retail customers from February 1992 to October 1996 and as an account manager for some of South Mill's major customers from March 1988 to February 1992. Prior to joining the company in March 1988, Ms. Grant worked as a buyer for two local retailers. Ms. Grant received a B.A. in humanities from the University of Georgia.

Robert T. Levitt has been vice president of operations since the company was incorporated in 1987. Prior to joining the company, Mr. Levitt was employed by the Fruit of the Loom company from 1975 to 1987, where he held various positions in manufacturing and labor relations. His last assignment was as the chief labor negotiator for the company. Mr. Levitt holds a B.S. in manufacturing technology from the University of Florida.

Nancy B. Dalton has been vice president of human resources and personnel since March of 1991, and as director of personnel since April of 1989. Prior to joining the company, she was a self-employed benefits consultant from August 1980 to April 1989. From May 1964 to August 1980, Ms. Dalton was a homemaker. Ms. Dalton received a certificate of personnel administration from DeKalb Community College.

Timothy H. Brooks has been controller since joining South Mill in July 1996. Mr. Brooks has more than seven years of experience in both public accounting and private industry. From January 1990 until July 1996, he was employed by Arthur Andersen as an auditor. Mr. Brooks received a B.S. in accounting from the University of Georgia and has passed the Uniform Certified Public Accounting exam.

To date, South Mill has not found it necessary to hire a full-time chief financial officer and has instead relied on Howard T. McBain, its president and chief executive officer, and the accounting firm of Arthur Andersen to manage the company's finances. In July 1996, South Mill hired Timothy H. Brooks to be its controller, but Mr. Brooks has had only limited involvement with the information presented in this plan. By the middle of 1998, South Mill intends to start a search for a chief financial officer.

Management compensation

Compensation for members of South Mill's management team is shown in the following table:

Name and position	Year	Salary	Bonus	Other
Howard T. McBain	1997	$65,000	$10,000	
President and Chief Executive Officer	1996	$62,000	$8,000	
Sally Grant	1997	$53,000	$8,000	
Vice President of Sales and Marketing	1996	$50,000	$6,000	
Robert F. Levitt	1997	$53,000	$8,000	
Vice President of Operations	1996	$50,000	$6,000	
Nancy B. Dalton	1997	$52,000	$5,000	
Vice President of Human Resources and Personnel	1996	$51,000	$4,000	
Timothy H. Brooks	1997	$43,000	$2,000	
Controller	1996	$41,000	NA	$19,500 *

* Represents reimbursement for relocation expenses.

Personnel

By December 31, 1997, South Mill had 83 full-time employees: nine of which were in sales and marketing; five in finance; eight in human resources and personnel; seven in administration; and 54 in manufacturing and operations. Occasionally, the company hires temporary employees to satisfy production needs in manufacturing and operations. Currently, the company does not have any collective bargaining agreements with any labor unions and considers its labor relations to be good. South Mill does all of its own recruiting, hiring, and training for factory personnel and occasionally makes use of a local headhunter for middle and upper management levels.

Part II. Financial Data

South Mill, Inc.
Pro forma balance sheet: Three-year summary
For the years ended December 31, 1998, 1999, and 2000

	1998	1999	2000
Assets			
Current assets			
Cash	$265,692	$699,956	$831,372
Accounts receivable	1,082,194	1,301,821	1,614,258
Income taxes receivable	0	0	0
Deferred income taxes	72,457	87,162	108,081
Inventory	1,633,237	1,964,696	2,436,223
Other current assets	30,124	36,238	44,935
Total current assets	3,083,704	4,089,873	5,034,869
Property, plant, and equipment			
Land	24,163	24,163	24,163
Land improvements	26,696	26,696	26,696
Buildings and improvements	844,353	844,353	844,353
Machinery and equipment	1,286,566	1,286,566	1,286,566
Total property, plant, and equipment	2,181,778	2,181,778	2,181,778
Less accumulated depreciation	838,464	1,008,627	1,250,697
Property, plant, and equipment, net	1,343,314	1,173,151	931,081
Other assets	27,632	33,240	41,218
Total assets	4,454,650	5,296,264	6,007,168
Liabilities and shareholders' equity			
Current liabilities			
Current portion of long-term debt	40,783	49,060	49,060
Notes payable	0	0	0
Accounts payable	213,924	257,339	319,100
Income taxes payable	17,832	21,451	26,599
Accrued expenses	164,216	197,543	244,953
Total current liabilities	436,755	525,393	639,712
Long-term debt	2,518,496	2,518,496	2,068,496
Deferred income taxes	170,726	205,374	174,568
Total liabilities	3,125,977	3,249,263	2,882,776
Total shareholders' equity	1,328,673	2,047,001	3,124,391
Total liabilities and shareholders' equity	4,454,650	5,296,264	6,007,168

South Mill, Inc.
Pro forma income statement: Three-year summary
For the years ended December 31, 1998, 1999, and 2000

	1998	1999	2000
Net sales revenue	$6,486,863	$9,405,954	$13,638,633
Cost of goods sold	5,068,186	7,348,872	10,655,865
Gross profit margin	1,418,677	2,057,082	2,982,768
Expenses			
Sales and administrative	413,364	454,707	500,178
Depreciation	227,040	329,209	477,354
Interest on long-term debt	142,104	206,045	298,765
Other expense	36,252	52,562	76,216
Total expenses	818,760	1,042,523	1,352,513
Income (loss) before taxes	599,917	1,014,559	1,630,255
Taxes	227,040	435,160	851,400
Net income (loss)	372,877	579,399	778,855

South Mill, Inc.
Pro forma statement of cash flows: Three-year summary
For the years ended December 31, 1998, 1999, and 2000

	1998	1999	2000
Net income	$372,877	$579,399	$778,855
Adjustments to reconcile net income to net cash provided			
Provision for depreciation and amortization	227,040	329,209	477,354
Other, net	0	0	0
Increase in accounts receivable	(198,612)	(219,627)	(312,437)
(Increase) decrease in income taxes receivable	42,600	0	0
(Increase) decrease in deferred income taxes	0	0	0
Increase in inventories	(337,685)	(331,459)	(471,527)
Increase (decrease) in accounts payable	100,000	43,415	61,761
Increase in accrued expenses	64,416	33,327	47,410
Increase (decrease) in notes payable	(80,506)	0	0
Net cash provided by (used in) operating activities	190,130	434,264	581,416
Cash flows from investing activities			
Purchases of property, plants, and equipment	(420,000)	0	0
Other, net	0	0	0
Net cash used in investing activities	(420,000)	0	0
Cash flow from financing activities			
Proceeds from issuance of long-term debt	500,000	0	(450,000)
Repayments of long-term debt	0	0	0
Net borrowings from (repayments of) revolving loan	0	0	0
Net cash provided by (used in) financing activities	500,000	0	(450,000)
Net increase (decrease) in cash	270,130	434,264	131,416

South Mill, Inc.
Pro forma ratio analysis: Three-year summary
For the years ended December 31, 1998, 1999, and 2000

	1998	1999	2000
Profitability ratios			
Return on equity (ROE)	28.06 %	28.30 %	24.93 %
Return on total investment	8.37 %	10.94 %	12.97 %
Net profit margin	5.75 %	6.16 %	5.71 %
Gross margin on sales	21.87 %	21.87 %	21.87 %
Liquidity ratios			
Working capital/current ratio	7.1	7.8	7.9
Quick ratio	3.1	3.8	3.8
Receivable turnover	6.0	7.2	8.4
Inventory turnover	3.1	3.7	4.4

Notes to Pro forma financial statements

Balance sheet
♦ Return on total investment, or net income divided by total assets, will improve from 8.37 percent in 1998 to 12.97 percent in 2000 because of the efficiencies obtained from the proposed plant expansion described in the statement of purpose.
♦ South Mill will be able to sell its inventory more rapidly because of improvements in its just-in-time delivery system. Its inventory turnover ratio will improve from 3.1 percent in 1998 to 4.4 percent in 2000.

Income statement
♦ The South Mill sales forecast of $6,486,863, $9,405,954, $13,638,633 in annual net revenue for the years ended 1998, 1999, and 2000, respectively, is based on obtaining the financing outlined in the statement of purpose and completing the described expansion during 1998.
♦ Cost of goods sold (COGS) is assumed to remain steady for 1998, 1999, and 2000 at 79 percent of sales. Similarly, the gross profit margin on sales will remain constant at 21 percent.

South Mill, Inc.
Pro forma balance sheet: Detail by month: 1998

	Jan	Feb	Mar	Apr	May	Jun	Jul	Aug	Sep	Oct	Nov	Dec	Total
Assets													
Current assets													
Cash	$24,020	$142,635	$174,653	$228,823	$250,768	$271,401	$191,499	$201,603	$222,450	$234,680	$242,653	$265,692	$265,692
Accounts receivable	900,132	916,683	933,234	949,785	966,336	982,887	999,438	1,015,989	1,032,540	1,049,091	1,065,642	1,082,193	1,082,193
Income taxes receivable	42,600	42,600	42,600	0	0	0	0	0	0	0	0	0	0
Deferred income taxes	92,484	92,484	92,484	72,457	72,457	72,457	72,457	72,457	72,457	72,457	72,457	72,457	72,457
Inventory	1,323,693	1,351,833	1,379,973	1,408,113	1,436,253	1,464,393	1,492,533	1,520,673	1,548,818	1,576,958	1,605,098	1,633,238	1,633,238
Other current assets	5,966	5,966	5,966	5,966	5,966	5,966	5,966	5,966	5,966	30,124	30,124	30,124	30,124
Total current assets	2,388,895	2,552,201	2,628,910	2,665,144	2,731,780	2,797,104	2,761,893	2,816,688	2,882,231	2,963,310	3,015,974	3,083,704	3,083,704
Property, plant, and equipment													
Land	24,163	24,163	24,163	24,163	24,163	24,163	24,163	24,163	24,163	24,163	24,163	24,163	24,163
Land improvements	26,696	26,696	26,696	26,696	26,696	26,696	26,696	26,696	26,696	26,696	26,696	26,696	26,696
Buildings and improvements	544,353	844,353	844,353	844,353	844,353	844,353	844,353	844,353	844,353	844,353	844,353	844,353	844,353
Machinery and equipment	1,166,566	1,286,566	1,286,566	1,286,566	1,286,566	1,286,566	1,286,566	1,286,566	1,286,566	1,286,566	1,286,566	1,286,566	1,286,566
Total property, plant, and equipment	1,761,778	2,181,778	2,181,778	2,181,778	2,181,778	2,181,778	2,181,778	2,181,778	2,181,778	2,181,778	2,181,778	2,181,778	2,181,778
Less accumulated depreciation	551,027	551,027	579,768	608,512	637,256	666,000	694,744	723,488	752,232	780,976	809,720	838,464	838,464
Property, plant, and equipment, net	1,210,751	1,630,751	1,602,010	1,573,266	1,544,522	1,515,778	1,487,034	1,458,290	1,429,546	1,400,802	1,372,058	1,343,314	1,343,314
Other assets	13,765	13,765	13,765	13,765	13,765	13,765	13,765	13,765	13,765	27,632	27,632	27,632	27,632
Total assets	3,613,411	4,196,717	4,244,685	4,252,175	4,290,067	4,326,647	4,262,692	4,288,743	4,325,542	4,391,744	4,415,664	4,454,650	4,454,650
Liabilities and shareholders' equity													
Current liabilities													
Current portion of long-term debt	34,218	34,218	34,870	35,527	36,184	36,841	37,498	38,155	38,812	39,469	40,126	40,783	40,783
Notes payable	80,506	80,506	80,506	80,506	80,506	80,506	0	0	0	0	0	0	0
Accounts payable	122,257	130,590	138,923	147,256	155,589	163,922	172,255	180,588	188,921	197,258	205,591	213,924	213,924
Income taxes payable	1,486	2,972	4,458	5,944	7,430	8,916	10,402	11,888	13,374	14,860	16,346	17,832	17,832
Accrued expenses	105,168	110,536	115,904	121,272	126,640	132,008	137,376	142,744	148,112	153,480	158,848	164,216	164,216
Total current liabilities	343,635	358,822	374,661	390,505	406,349	422,193	357,531	373,375	389,219	405,067	420,911	436,755	436,755
Long-term debt	2,018,496	2,518,496	2,518,496	2,518,496	2,518,496	2,518,496	2,518,496	2,518,496	2,518,496	2,518,496	2,518,496	2,518,496	2,518,496
Deferred income taxes	170,726	170,726	170,726	170,726	170,726	170,726	170,726	170,726	170,726	170,726	170,726	170,726	170,726
Total liabilities	2,532,857	3,048,044	3,063,883	3,079,727	3,095,571	3,111,415	3,046,753	3,062,597	3,078,441	3,094,289	3,110,133	3,125,977	3,125,977
Total shareholders' equity	1,080,554	1,148,673	1,180,802	1,172,448	1,194,496	1,215,232	1,215,939	1,226,146	1,247,101	1,297,455	1,305,531	1,328,673	1,328,673
Total liabilities and shareholders' equity	3,613,411	4,196,717	4,244,685	4,252,175	4,290,067	4,326,647	4,262,692	4,288,743	4,325,542	4,391,744	4,415,664	4,454,650	4,454,650

South Mill, Inc.
Pro forma income statement
Detail by month: 1998

	Jan	Feb	Mar	Apr	May	Jun	Jul	Aug	Sep	Oct	Nov	Dec	Total
Net sales revenue	$594,629	$599,629	$589,629	$537,572	$543,572	$537,572	$487,429	$489,429	$538,572	$540,572	$479,686	$548,572	$6,486,863
Cost of goods sold	464,584	468,490	460,677	420,005	424,693	420,005	380,828	382,391	420,786	422,349	374,779	428,599	5,068,186
Gross profit margin	130,045	131,139	128,952	117,567	118,879	117,567	106,601	107,038	117,786	118,223	104,907	119,973	1,418,677
Expenses													
Sales and administrative	34,447	34,447	34,447	34,447	34,447	34,447	34,447	34,447	34,447	34,447	34,447	34,447	413,364
Depreciation	13,050	13,050	20,094	20,094	20,094	20,094	20,094	20,094	20,094	20,094	20,094	20,094	227,040
Interest on long-term debt	8,167	8,167	12,577	12,577	12,577	12,577	12,577	12,577	12,577	12,577	12,577	12,577	142,104
Other expense (income)	9,063	0	0	9,063	0	0	9,063	0	0	9,063	0	0	36,252
Total expenses	64,727	55,664	67,118	76,181	67,118	67,118	76,181	67,118	67,118	76,181	67,118	67,118	818,760
Income (loss) before taxes	65,318	75,475	61,834	41,386	51,761	50,449	30,420	39,920	50,668	42,042	37,789	52,855	599,917
Taxes	18,920	18,920	18,920	18,920	18,920	18,920	18,920	18,920	18,920	18,920	18,920	18,920	227,040
Net income (loss)	46,398	56,555	42,914	22,466	32,841	31,529	11,500	21,000	31,748	23,122	18,869	33,935	372,877

South Mill, Inc.
Pro forma statement of cash flows
Detail by month: 1998

	Jan	Feb	Mar	Apr	May	Jun	Jul	Aug	Sep	Oct	Nov	Dec	Total
Net income	$46,398	$56,555	$42,914	$22,466	$32,841	$31,529	$11,500	$21,000	$31,748	$23,122	$18,869	$33,935	$372,877
Adjustments to reconcile net income to net cash provided													
Provision for depreciation and amortization	13,050	13,050	20,094	20,094	20,094	20,094	20,094	20,094	20,094	20,094	20,094	20,094	227,040
Other, net	0	0	0	0	0	0	0	0	0	0	0	0	0
Increase in accounts receivable	(16,551)	(16,551)	(16,551)	(16,551)	(16,551)	(16,551)	(16,551)	(16,551)	(16,551)	(16,551)	(16,551)	(16,551)	(198,612)
(Increase) decrease in income taxes receivable	0	0	0	42,600	0	0	0	0	0	0	0	0	42,600
(Increase) decrease in deferred income taxes	0	0	0	0	0	0	0	0	0	0	0	0	0
Increase in inventories	(28,140)	(28,140)	(28,140)	(28,140)	(28,140)	(28,140)	(28,140)	(28,140)	(28,145)	(28,140)	(28,140)	(28,140)	(337,685)
Increase (decrease) in accounts payable	8,333	8,333	8,333	8,333	8,333	8,333	8,333	8,333	8,333	8,337	8,333	8,333	100,000
Increase in accrued expenses	5,368	5,368	5,368	5,368	5,368	5,368	5,368	5,368	5,368	5,368	5,368	5,368	64,416
Increase (decrease) in notes payable	0	0	0	0	0	0	(80,506)	0	0	0	0	0	(80,506)
Net cash provided by (used in) operating activities	28,458	38,615	32,018	54,170	21,945	20,633	(79,902)	10,104	20,847	12,230	7,973	23,039	190,130
Cash flows from investing activities													
Purchases of property, plant, and equipment	0	(420,000)	0	0	0	0	0	0	0	0	0	0	(420,000)
Other, net	0	0	0	0	0	0	0	0	0	0	0	0	0
Net cash used in investing activities	0	(420,000)	0	0	0	0	0	0	0	0	0	0	(420,000)
Cash flow from financing activities													
Proceeds from issuance of long-term debt	0	500,000	0	0	0	0	0	0	0	0	0	0	500,000
Repayments of long-term debt	0	0	0	0	0	0	0	0	0	0	0	0	0
Net borrowings from (repayments of) revolving loan	0	0	0	0	0	0	0	0	0	0	0	0	0
Net cash provided by (used in) financing activities	0	500,000	0	0	0	0	0	0	0	0	0	0	500,000
Net increase (decrease) in cash	28,458	118,615	32,018	54,170	21,945	20,633	(79,902)	10,104	20,847	12,230	7,973	23,039	270,130

- Net profit margin, or net income divided by net sales revenue, will be 6 percent for 1998, 1999, and 2000. This will result in net income more than doubling from 1998 to 2000, or rising from $372,877 to $778,855, with the corresponding increase in sales revenue.

Cash flow

- The company anticipates receiving the $500,000 for its proposed plant expansion in February 1998. It also plans to complete the expansion in the same month.
- As a result of the company's continued growth, South Mill will use some of the cash received from its loan to increase inventory by $28,140. However, some of the increase in inventory will be offset by corresponding increases in accounts payable of $8,333.
- The company will also pay off its notes payable of $80,506 in July 1998.

Part II

Create a Better Business Plan by Using the Internet

Chapter 12

Overview of the Internet Resource Guide

The widespread availability of the Internet and World Wide Web gives you the opportunity to improve your business plan by accessing current marketing, managerial, and financial information. Previously, most of this information was available only through back issues of magazines, public libraries, and government archives. Now it can be obtained on personal computers at home or in the office.

Not only can you access statistical, financial, and economic data with the Internet, you can also find plenty of advice on:

◆ Business plan outlines.

◆ Market research.

◆ Target marketing.

◆ Choosing a franchise.

◆ Selecting a location.

◆ Advertising strategies.

◆ Obtaining bank loans.

◆ Raising venture capital.

The remainder of this book covers Web sites that you can access through the Internet to improve your business plan. Unlike the first part of the book, which was designed to help individuals with little or no business planning experience to understand the fundamentals of business planning, this part deals exclusively with Web sites that will be useful in creating your business plan.

This part of the book assumes that you are already online—that you are connected to the Internet and know how to use a Web browser, such as Netscape or Internet Explorer. It also assumes that you are familiar enough with URLs (www.sitename.com) that you can enter them in your Web browser's address box as they are shown on the following pages.

How to use these Internet chapters

The structure of the following chapters is essentially the same. Five to 10 of the most relevant sites pertaining to the chapter title are reviewed at the beginning of the chapter. This includes the name of the article, or source of data, with a corresponding URL. Immediately following this is the name of the company or organization that is responsible for maintaining this information, and its associated URL. For instance, the following information is presented for the article titled "Creating an effective business plan," which can be found on the American Express Web site.

Creating an effective business plan

http://www6.americanexpress.com/smallbusiness/resources/starting/biz_plan/
index.shtml?aexp_nav=sbs_hp_bizplan

American Express
http://www6.americanexpress.com/smallbusiness

Following the company name (and URL) responsible for maintaining the Web site, is a brief synopsis of the article or data. At the end of this synopsis you will find step-by-step instructions on how to access the information. For instance, to access the previous Web site, you could begin by entering the American Express Small Business Web pages, and then performing a series of mouse clicks and scrolling operations to get to the article titled "Creating an effective business plan." Or you could simply enter the entire URL for the article and skip the instructions.

Visualize the chapter layouts as follows:

Title of article or data

URL

Company, or organization, responsible for the article or data
URL

Brief synopsis

Instructions to locate the article or data

At the end of every chapter, you will find a series of additional Web sites with associated URLs and brief descriptions that might also be helpful in creating your business plan.

The dynamics of the Web and additional help

The World Wide Web is a very dynamic, or constantly changing, environment. As such, you must recognize that some of the sites reviewed in this part of the book will have changed by the time you begin the process of creating your business plan. Therefore, every effort has been made to provide you with as much information as possible to facilitate the location of these Web sites.

All of the Web sites and instructions contained in this book were reviewed and updated during September 1998. However, between then and now, Web masters will have changed the look or location of some of their Web pages. Further, some of the sites may have disappeared altogether. This is one of the reasons two Web addresses have been included for many of the sites (the home page and actual location of the article). If the instructions have become outdated, try typing the URL for the specific article directly into your Web browser's address box.

Additionally, an updated list of business planning Web sites can be found at:

Additional Online Business Planning Help
http://members.aol.com/Bobandbri/onlinebp.html

E-mail address
bobandbri@aol.com

If you send an email, make sure to include the words Online Business Planning, or OBP, in the subject text.

Recommended sites

Although the Internet already includes thousands of Web sites that can help you with your business plan, there are a few that you should definitely review as you go through the following chapters.

U.S. Small Business Administration
http://www.sbaonline.sba.gov

Provides a wealth of business planning advice, including business plan outlines, preparing financial statements, and how to apply for SBA loans.

IPO Central
http://www.ipocentral.com

Has daily listings of initial public offerings with corresponding links to EDGAR Online. Use this site to compare your business with others that are going public (selling stock).

Inc. Magazine
http://www.inc.com

Through the magazine's archives, you can get plenty of advice by reading articles that were published in past issues.

Business Week Magazine
http://www.businessweek.com

Publishes a yearly listing of "Hot Growth Companies" with descriptions of their management, growth strategies, and industry positioning.

American List Counsel
http://www.amlist.com

Provides lists of all of the companies and households in the United States. Excellent source for market segmentation and competitive analysis data.

FranInfo
http://www.franinfo.com

One of the many sites that offers information on purchasing a franchise.

Industry Research Desk
http://www.virtualpet.com/industry/rdindex2.htm

Learn how to analyze your industry with the 13-step plan provided by the Industry Research Desk.

Business Research Lab
http://www.busreslab.com

If you have never conducted any primary market research, or you want to learn more, try the Business Research Lab Web site for plenty of practical advice.

SalesDoctors Magazine
http://salesdoctors.com

Provides a series of articles than can help you improve your advertising and promotion.

American Society for Training and Development
http://www.astd.org/index.html

For information on training your employees, start with the American Society for Training and Development.

BenefitsLink
http://www.benefitslink.com

Has a search engine and bulletin board to help you get answers to any questions regarding employee benefits.

Venture Capital
http://www.once.com/gcg/

A complete online book about venture capital.

Chapter 13

Business Plan Outlines

In their book, *Your First Business Plan* (Sourcebooks, 1995), Joseph Covello and Brian Hazelgren state, "A business plan helps entrepreneurs and business managers to think through their strategies, balance their enthusiasm with facts, and recognize their limitations. It will help you avoid potentially disastrous errors like undercapitalizing, creating negative cash flow, hiring the wrong people, selecting the wrong location, and pursuing the wrong market....A business owner who fails to plan, plans to fail."

All business plans start with an outline that must cover certain aspects of the proposed business, including a description of the business, the marketing strategy, the management team, and a financial plan.

This chapter begins with a review of the business plan outline contained on the Small Business Administration (SBA) Web site. This site provides an excellent template for getting started and serves as the outline for topics covered in this book.

Business plans

http://www.sbaonline.sba.gov/starting/businessplan.html

U.S. Small Business Administration
http://www.sbaonline.sba.gov

The U.S. Small Business Administration (SBA) is a government agency formed by Congress to help entrepreneurs create and manage successful businesses. With offices in every state, the SBA provides advice, training, and financing for business owners.

Through its extensive Web site, the SBA delivers an excellent business plan outline for you to follow as you develop your business plan. According to the SBA, a business plan consists of four distinct sections:

1. Description of the business.
2. Marketing plan.
3. Financial management plan.
4. Management plan.

Additionally, the SBA indicates that a business plan should include an executive summary, supporting documents, and financial projections.

To view the SBA business plan outline with all of its elements, do the following:

1. In your browser's address box, type http://www.sbaonline.sba.gov and press Enter.
2. After the SBA home page appears, scroll down and click on the [Starting] button.
3. On the next page, locate and click on the [Business Plans] button.
4. Now you can review the entire SBA Business Plan Outline by scrolling down the screen.

Creating an effective business plan

http://www6.americanexpress.com/smallbusiness/resources/starting/biz_plan/index.shtml?aexp_nav=sbs_hp_bizplan

American Express
http://www6.americanexpress.com/smallbusiness

The American Express Web site, through its "Small Business Exchange" section, provides business planning and marketing advice for entrepreneurs. One area that is especially useful is the "Business Plan Workshop," because it provides an interactive business plan outline for a ficticious company.

According to American Express, "This workshop will help you create a business plan to guide your business through the startup or growth phase, a search for capital, or any other endeavor your small business undertakes." The business plan outline is divided into the following seven elements:

1. Introductory Elements.
2. Business Description.
3. The Market.
4. Development & Production.
5. Sales & Marketing.
6. Management.
7. Financials.

To access the "Business Plan Workshop," do the following:

1. Type http://www6.americanexpress.com/smallbusiness in your Web browser's address box and press Enter.
2. On the Small Business Exchange screen, click on [Create a Business Plan].

3. On the Creating an Effective Business Plan screen, scroll down and you will now be able to select from the one of the seven elements for more information.

Business plan for a startup business

http://web.miep.org/bus_plan/plan.html

Network for Excellence in Manufacturing Online
http://www.nemonline.org

The Network for Excellence in Manufacturing Online (NEM Online) Web site was developed by Michigan State University "to support the activities of manufacturing assistance providers and manufacturers in the state of Michigan." Although NEM Online Web site has a manufacturing focus, the wide variety of business planning information is useful for entrepreneurs in any business.

The Business Plan section provides a series of templates that will help you to prepare your plan, including Statement of Purpose, Business Information, Description of Business, Personnel, Market Analysis, Financial, and Supporting Documents. "When you have completed all the templates, then you will have a draft business plan. Rewrite this draft in final copy format for presentation to lenders, creditors, investors, employees, and anyone else to whom you wish to give information about your business development project."

To get to the business plan section, do the following:

1. Type http://web.miep.org/bus_plan/plan.html in your browsers address box and press Enter.

How to develop and use a business plan

http://www.edgeonline.com/main/bizbuilders/biz/sm_business/busplan.shtml

Edward Lowe Foundation
http://www.lowe.org/mission.htm

The Edward Lowe Foundation (ELF), a nonprofit organization founded by Edward Lowe, delivers business information and research through its site on the Web. "Ed Lowe envisioned that his foundation would live in perpetuity and help assure the future of the free enterprise system."

"The Entrepreneurial Edge Online Business Builders," contained within ELF, provides a training module on "How to Develop and Use a Business Plan." This module will show you the steps required to develop a complete business plan for potential investors. This business plan outline includes:

♦ Begin The Plan With a Summary.
♦ Describe Your Company.
♦ Analyze Your Market and Determine Your Strategy.

- Describe Your Products/Services and How They Are Produced.
- Describe Your Management Organization.
- Develop Your Financial Forecast.
- Determine Your Proposed Financing.
- Outline Your Plan(s) for the Future.
- Other Considerations.

To view the ELF business plan outline, do the following:

1. Type http://www.lowe.org in your browser's address box and press Enter.
2. On the ELF home page click on the Entrepreneurial Edge Online box.
3. From the Edge Online page, select interactive modules.
4. Once you have arrived at the Edge Online Business Builders page, scroll down to the Small Business Practices section and click on Develop and use a business plan under the Small Business Practices heading.

Writing an effective business plan

http://www.dtonline.com/writing/wrcover.htm

Deloitte & Touche LLP
http://www.dtonline.com

Deloitte and Touche, a professional services firm that specializes in accounting, auditing, tax, and management services, has an extensive Web site that offers entrepreneurs plenty of advice. This site is quick to point out that "presentation of the story is crucial to your success. A good business plan conveys your company's prospects and growth potential, helping you attract financing and other resources."

The Deloitte and Touche Web site provides an entire section on writing an effective business plan. This plan gives you the opportunity to "tell prospective investors about your firm's marketing plan, financial condition, and more." The business plan outline contained on this site is broken down into 11 sections, as follows: Table of Contents, Overview, The Need for Planning, The Business Plan Process, The Executive Summary; The Company, Strategy & Management; The Market; The Product or Service; Sales and Promotion; Financial Information; and Putting It All Together.

To view "Writing an effective business plan," do the following:

1. Type http://www.dtonline.com in your Web browser's address box and press Enter.
2. Scroll down the page and click on Site Search.

3. On the Site Search page, type "Business Plan" in the search box and press Enter.
4. After you reach the Search Results page, scroll down and select <u>Writing an Effective Business Plan</u>.

Planning fundamentals

http://www.sb.gov.bc.ca/smallbus/workshop/market/whyplan.html

Canada/British Columbia Business Service Centre
http://www.sb.gov.bc.ca/smallbus/sbhome.html

The Canada/British Columbia Business Service Centre (BCBSC), provided by the Ministry of Small Business, Tourism and Culture Services and Programs for Small Business, "delivers a wide range of services for small business throughout British Columbia." Like the U.S. Small Business Administration, the Ministry offers financing, information, and publications for businesses.

The BCBSC compares running a business with flying an airplane. An entrepreneur who lacks a detailed, well-researched business plan is as likely to crash as an experienced pilot who flies a risky mission without a detailed, well-researched flight plan. The BCBSC Web site has a detailed business plan outline that covers the following elements:

- Title Page
- Executive Summary
- Table of Contents
- The Business Venture
- The Company; Management
- The Product
- The Market Place
- Market Size
- The Competition
- Sales Plan
- Sales Forecast
- Sources of Market Information
- Product Development
- Production
- Product Cost
- Gross Profit
- Financial Requirements
- Pro Forma Income Statements
- Cash Flow Projections

To the see the BCBSC sample business plan, do the following:

1. Type http://www.sb.gov.bc.ca/smallbus/sbhome.html in your browser's address box and press Enter.
2. On the BCBSC home page select <u>On line Small Business Workshop</u>.
3. After you reach the On line Small Business Workshop page, click on <u>Sample Business Plan</u> under the Planning Fundamentals heading to see the entire outline.

Additional planning resources

Here are a few other business planning resources that you may find useful as you develop your outline:

IPO Central
http://www.ipocentral.com

Has daily listings of initial public offerings with corresponding links to EDGAR Online. Use this site to compare your business with others that are going public (selling stock).

MoneyHunter
http://www.moneyhunter.com/htm/btemp.htm

The MoneyHunter Web site provides a business plan template that is described as "the must-have document for raising money to start, grow, or buy a business."

Palo Alto Software Inc.
http://pasware.com/html/free_stuff.htm

The Palo Alto Software site has two sample business plan outlines that you can browse through online. According to Palo Alto, "Both of these sample plans are based on actual business plans that were approved by investors."

Business Resource Center
http://www.morebusiness.com/templates/busplan/

Provides sample business plans and templates in the Business Plan and Press Releases section.

Arthur Andersen
http://www.benlore.com/files/emexpert1_2.html

On the Benlore Web site, the Arthur Andersen Emerging Business Consulting group "describes the strategy to creating an effective business plan."

Service Corps of Retired Executives
http://www.scn.org/civic/score-online

SCORE has 12,300 volunteers nationwide who provide advice to entrepreneurs and small-business owners. You may ask questions about your business plan through an e-mail or toll-free number.

eWeb
http://www.slu.edu/eweb/bplan1.htm

Produced by the Saint Louis University School of Business and Administration, this site provides many useful links under Business Planning located on its home page.

Small Business Innovative Research
http://www.sbir.dsu.edu/home/proposal_preparation/outline.htm

Plans submitted by technology-based small businesses to obtain funding from federal agencies.

bplans.com!
http://www.bplans.com/index1.html

Provides sample business plans for retailers, service companies, and mixed companies on its Web site.

Chapter 14

Legal Structures for Business

As we pointed out in Chapter 2, sole proprietorship is easy to set up, does not require any legal form of business organization, and requires the least amount of tax reporting to state and federal agencies. On the other hand, incorporating your business is not easy to set up and requires expert legal advice and significant resources to prepare tax returns, but it provides limited liability for the owners in the event of a lawsuit.

The four types of legal structures are sole proprietorships, partnerships, corporations, and limited liability companies. Your selection should be based on the goals of the business and consider the tax and personal liability consequences that are unique to each legal structure. Consult an attorney and be aware of the documents that must be filed with federal, state, and local governments. This chapter reviews Web sites that cover legal structures for business, sites where you can seek additional legal help, and sites that offer tax advice.

Legal formation of your business

http://www.ecodev.state.mo.us/mbac/legal/4types.htm

Missouri Business Assistance Center (MBAC)
http://www.ecodev.state.mo.us/mbac/body.htm

The Missouri Business Assistance Center (MBAC) helps business owners and entrepreneurs "obtain the proper permits, licenses, state sales/use tax accounts, a federal employer identification number, and other miscellaneous business permits." Although this Web site is designed for businesses in Missouri, the legal structures section can be applied to virtually any state in the country.

Through the MBAC Web site, you will learn about the four primary types of business structures. The site also contains information on other types of structures, such as Subchapter S Corporations and Not-for-Profit

Corporations. To visit the MBAC site and learn more about business legal structures, complete the following steps:

1. In your browser's address box, type http://www.ecodev.state.mo.us/mbac/body.htm and press Enter.
2. After the MBAC home page appears, scroll down and select the [Legal Formation] button.
3. On the next page, locate and click on 4 types of Business Structures.

Advantages and disadvantages of incorporating

http://www.corporate.com/html/information.html

Business Incorporating Guide
http://www.corporate.com

The Business Incorporating Guide Web site, created by Corporate Agents, Inc., "contains everything you need to form a new corporation or limited liability company in any state for as little as $11, plus state filing fees." Simply fill out the form online and submit it through the Web site.

However, before you decide to set up a corporation, make sure you read the entire discussion contained on this Web site concerning the advantages and disadvantages of a corporate legal structure over a sole proprietorship. You should also consult an attorney before you reach a final decision.

To visit the Business Incorporating Guide site, do the following:

1. In your browser's address box, type http://www.corporate.com and press Enter.
2. On the Guide's home page, click on [Everything You Need to Know].
3. You will now be able to select the following topics: Advantages of Incorporating; Disadvantages of Incorporating, Costs, Types of Corporations, and International Incorporating.

Lawyer referral services

http://www.abanet.org/referral/home.html

American Bar Association (ABA)
http://www.abanet.org

Before finalizing the legal structure for your business, it is important that you review your plans with an attorney. The American Bar Association (ABA) is the "largest voluntary professional association in the world with a membership of more than 380,000" lawyers, associates, and law students. The ABA Web site provides a referral service to help you locate an attorney.

Lawyer referral services are run by state and local bar associations, and can assist you in locating a lawyer specializing in legal structures for business. Because lawyer referral is a public service, do not expect any legal advice or free legal services.

To access the ABA home page and locate a referral service in your area try the following steps:

1. In your browser's address box, type http://www.abanet.org and press Enter.
2. After the ABA home page appears, click on the [Public Information] button.
3. On the public information page, scroll down to the Legal Assistance heading and click on Lawyer Referral.
4. On the Lawyer Referral Services page, scroll down and select the state in which you are planning to start your business.
5. You are now presented with a list of referral services, including the address and phone number, that you can contact.

Law links

http://www.ioma.com/directory/law/index.shtml

Institute of Management and Administration
http://www.ioma.com/index.html

The Institute of Management and Administration (IOMA) publishes "print and electronic newsletters to save business people time...and money." Its Web site covers a wide variety of subjects that are of interest to business owners, including links to multiple law-related Web sites. For instance, if you were looking for the Trade Law Library and did not know the URL, then you might try the IOMA section on Law.

To access the IOMA Web site, do the following:

1. In your browser's address box, type http://www.ioma.com/index.html and press Enter.
2. On the IOMA home page, click on [Business Directory].
3. On the business directory page, click on Law under the Jump to Links heading.
4. You will now be able to access a variety of law sites, including Lawyers Online.

Business taxpayer information

http://www.irs.ustreas.gov/prod/search/site_tree.html

Internal Revenue Service
http://www.irs.ustreas.gov/prod/cover.html

At the Internal Revenue Service (IRS) Web site you will find tax tips to help your business. More than 600 forms, publications, and instructions can be downloaded to your computer. One IRS site you will want to look at is the

"Business Taxpayer Info," which provides "tax information for business tax-payers; sole proprietor, partnership, or corporation. 'Where To File' and 'Around the Nation' will help you find information specific to your state."

In addition, contact the state in which you are planning to start your business and obtain the necessary tax instructions. Try the "Where to File State Information" in the Topic Links window.

To visit the IRS site and review the "Business Taxpayer Info" section, do the following:

1. In your browser's address box, type http://www.irs.ustreas. gov/prod/cover.html and press Enter.
2. On the Digital Daily page, scroll to the bottom and select <u>Site Tree</u>.
3. From the Topic Index heading, scroll down and click on <u>Business Taxpayer Info</u>.
4. Then in the Tax Info For Business Links window, select <u>Business Tax Kit</u>.
5. The Business Tax Kit is a packet of federal forms and publications that is available to those who apply for Employer Identification Numbers. It includes the 1295 Form SS-4 Application for Employer Identification Number.

State tax information

http://www.taxweb.com/state/index.html

TaxWeb
http://www.taxweb.com

TaxWeb provides information on federal, state, and local tax-related developments. It will give you answers to general tax questions, "plus links to current federal and state-sponsored tax sites to allow more comprehensive tax research."

Follow these directions:

1. In your browser's address box, type http://www.taxweb. com and press Enter.
2. Scroll down the screen and click on the [State Links] button.
3. On the State Tax Information page, select a state about which you would like more tax information.
4. At the TaxWeb page for a particular state, you will be able to select the state home page, the governor's home page, or many direct links to state tax information.

Additional legal resources

The following are a few more legal resources that you may find helpful as you set up the legal structure for your business.

Court TV Small Business Law Center
http://www.courttv.com/legalhelp/business

The Court TV Law Center has a Small Business Law Center that includes Web pages for forms and model documents, a directory to locate a lawyer, and seminars and discussions.

West's Legal Directory
http://www.wld.com/client/Welcome.asp

Search through 800,000-plus listings of lawyers and law firms in West's Legal Directory.

Practicing Attorney's Home Page
http://www.legalethics.com/pa/main.html

The Practicing Attorney's Home Page offers a searchable set of links (and brief descriptions) to all primary Internet legal resources.

American Arbitration Association
http://www.adr.org

The American Arbitration Association's (ADR) Web site, provides information about mediation, arbitration, and other forms of dispute resolution. According to ADR, mediation can help a company reduce legal expenses, manage disputes, and maintain business relationships.

Villanova Center for Information Law and Policy
http://www.cilp.org/tblhome.html

The Center for Information Law and Policy (CILP), is a joint effort between the Villanova University School of Law and the Chicago-Kent College of Law and provides an abundance of legal information for business.

CorpAmerica
http://www.corpamerica.com/incorporate.html

An additional resource for online incorporations.

Chapter 15

Business Types and Industry Research

Describing your business generically or by type is important because it provides an indication of how many competitors there are in your industry. If you were thinking of starting a retail store to sell baseball cards and other sports memorabilia, then you would find that there are nearly 8,000 stores nationwide performing the same function. A restauranteur would find more than 350,000 competitors nationwide, and a manufacturer of women's clothing would have nearly 6,000 competitors.

The U.S. Department of Commerce established the Standard Industrial Classification (SIC) coding system to provide numeric codes for all types of business in the country. The SIC codes separate the function of every business into 10 broad categories, including agriculture, mining, construction, manufacturing, communication, wholesale, retail, finance, services and government. These broad categories contain numerous subdivisions. For instance, there are more than 350 types of retail establishments that range from lumber yards, to yogurt stores, to shops that specialize in baseball cards.

This chapter provides instructions for accessing Web sites that will help you categorize your proposed business and industry.

SIC code list

http://www.amlist.com/abrowse.htm#sic

American List Counsel (ALC)
http://www.amlist.com

American List Counsel (ALC) helps companies create successful direct mail campaigns using databases that can often be sorted by SIC code. Additionally, the ALC Web site provides a complete description and breakdown of SIC codes. The 10 major industry groups that can be viewed on this site are as follows:

01-09: Agriculture, Forestry & Fishing
10-14: Mining
15-17: Contractors/Construction

20-39: Manufacturing

40-49: Communication, Transportation & Utilities

50-51: Wholesalers

52-59: Retailers

60-67: Finance, Insurance & Real Estate

70-89: Services

90-99: Government

By clicking on any of these categories, you can see the SIC numbers, industry names, and list counts for each.

To see the ALC listing of SIC codes, do the following:

1. Type http://www.amlist.com in your Web browser's address box and press Enter.
2. Click on the [ALC List Directory] button.
3. On the ALC List Directory page, select by SIC codes.
4. Scroll down the page and choose one of the SIC categories.

Introduction to Standard Industrial Classification codes

http://www.ssisamples.com/ssi.x2o$ssi_gen.search_item?id=23

Survey Sampling, Inc.

http://www.ssisamples.com/

Survey Sampling supports market researchers, pollsters, and survey organizations by providing sample data for research studies. Its Web site provides a brief introduction to Standard Industrial Classification (SIC) codes. These four-digit codes will help you to define your type of business in a format that is familiar to the federal government and other businesses. They will also help you to identify competitors and potential customers.

For more information, do the following:

1. Type: http://www.ssisamples.com in your Web browser's address box and press Enter.
2. On the Survey Sampling, Inc., home page, type Standard Industrial Classification in the site search box and press Enter.
3. On the SSI search results page, click on Business SIC Codes / Two-Digit Groups.
4. You will now see an entire breakdown of the codes, and on the Next Page there is a complete description of how they can be used.

North American Industry Classification System (NAICS)

http://www.census.gov/epcd/www/naics.html

U.S. Census Bureau

http://www.census.gov

SIC codes are maintained by the the U.S. Census Bureau, the data collection agency of the federal government. The current system is being replaced by the North American Industry Classification System (NAICS), to make structural improvements and identify more than 350 new industries. "NAICS was developed jointly by the U.S., Canada, and Mexico to provide new comparability in statistics about business activity across North America."

For more information about NAICS, do the following:

1. In your Web browser's address box, type http://www.census.gov and press Enter.
2. On the Census Bureau home page, select the [Subjects A-Z] button.
3. After you reach the Subjects A-Z page, click on N in the Select an initial letter box.
4. You will then be able to select North American Industry Classification System for a complete description.

How NAICS will affect data users

http://www.census.gov/epcd/www/naicsusr.html

U.S. Census Bureau

http://www.census.gov

Under the new NAICS, industries are identified by a six-digit code, as opposed to the old four-digit SIC code. The new codes reflect "developments such as fiber optic cable manufacturing, satellite communications, and the reproduction of computer software, and changes in the way business is done: bed and breakfast inns, environmental consulting, warehouse clubs, pet supply stores, credit card issuing, diet and weight reduction centers."

To see some of the new industries now being identified by the NAICS, do the following:

1. In your Web browser's address box, type http://www.census.gov and press Enter.
2. On the Census Bureau home page, select the [Subjects A-Z] button.
3. After you reach the Subjects A-Z page, click on N in the Select an initial letter box.
4. Under the N heading, select North American Industry Classification System.
5. On the NAICS page, under the How NAICS will affect data users, select New industries.

Industry profiles

http://www.sbaer.uca.edu/sbaer/publications/index.html

Small Business Advancement National Center (SBANC)
http://www.sbaer.uca.edu/

The Small Business Advancement National Center (SBANC), located on the campus of the University of Central Arkansas, offers small business counseling and an electronic resource information center. The SBANC Web site contains a series of "Industry-Small Business Profiles" prepared by Small Business Institutes. There are more than 30 profiles that include antique shops, automotive industry, bicycle shops, childcare, fruit farms, hotels and motels, street vendors, and typing services.

To see the "Industry Profiles," do the following:

1. In your Web browser's address box, type http://www.sbaer.uca.edu and press Enter.
2. On the SBANC home page, scroll down and click on [Industry Profiles].
3. On the Small Business Publications page, select Industry Profiles.
4. You will now be able to choose from any of the 33 industry profiles listed.

How to learn about an industry or a specific company

http://www.virtualpet.com/industry/howto/search.htm

Industry Research Desk
http://www.virtualpet.com/industry/rdindex2.htm

The Industry Research Desk, a Web site maintained by Polson Enterprises, "provides tools for researching specific companies, industries, and manufacturing processes." For instance, the "How to Learn About an Industry or a Specific Company" section has a 13-step procedure you can follow to complete a thorough study on different business types.

To access the Industry Research Desk, do the following:

1. Type http://www.virtualpet.com/industry/rdindex2.htm in your Web browser's address box and press Enter.
2. On the Industry Research Desk page, select How to Learn About an Industry or a Specific Company and then follow the onscreen instructions.

Additional business type and industry research resources

Here are a few other Web pages that you may find useful as you research the different types of businesses and industries:

U.S. Industrial Outlook
http://www.ita.doc.gov/industry/otea/usio/usio95.html

The U.S. Global Trade Outlook, 1995-2000: Toward the 21st Century is published by the International Trade Administration.

U.S. Industry & Trade Outlook '98
http://www.ita.doc.gov/industry/otea/usito98/factshet.htm

Also produced by the International Trade Administration, the *Outlook 1998* provides an "industry-by-industry overview of the U.S. economy." This site contains a fact sheet. The entire document can be purchased from the U.S. Department of Commerce, or check your local library.

Federal Marketplace
http://www.fedmarket.com/sic/index.html

In addition to providing a complete listing of SIC codes, this site offers "assistance to companies in marketing and selling products and services to the federal government."

University of Washington
http://weber.u.washington.edu/~dev/sic.html

Another source for Standard Industrial Classification (SIC) codes.

Immigration Central
http://www.wave.net/upg/immigration/sic_index.html

Download the SIC codes to your PC from this site for a fee.

U.S. Census Bureau
http://www.census.gov/ftp/pub/cir/www/

From the U.S. Census Bureau, see an assortment of "Industry Reports" that can even be downloaded to your spreadsheet for further analysis.

National Directory of Magazines
http://www.mediafinder.com/mag_home.cfm

For current reading on your industry try the National Directory of Magazines. Created by Oxbridge Communications, this is one of the largest databases of print media in existense.

Chapter 16

Product and Service Benefits

As we discussed in Chapter 3, successful products and services aren't sold based on features, but on benefits: Light beer is less filling. Flame broiling tastes better. Skin cream can make you look younger.

As you begin to explore introducing a new product or service, or starting a new business, consideration must be given to the benefits being offered to potential consumers. Customers don't buy product and service features, they buy product and service benefits.

This chapter walks you through several Web sites that will help you describe your product and service benefits. Additionally, it reviews sites that contain information on obtaining patents.

Describe your products/services and how they are produced

http://www.edgeonline.com/main/bizbuilders/biz/sm_business/busplan.shtml

Edward Lowe Foundation

http://www.lowe.org/mission.htm

In addition to the business plan outline described in an earlier chapter, the Edward Lowe Foundation (ELF) Web site provides a brief narrative on how you should describe your products and services. You can find this material in "How to Develop and Use a Business Plan," under "The Entrepreneurial Edge Online Business Builders" module.

The advice from ELF is that you should "describe your product/service in layman's terms. Explain any niche you may have. Discuss your competitive advantage—why people will choose your product over your competitors', the benefits of your product/service, and how you will sustain your edge."

For the entire article on describing your products and services, do the following:

1. Type http://www.lowe.org in your browser's address box and press Enter.

2. On the ELF home page, click on [Entrepreneurial EdgeOnline].

3. From the Entrepreneurial EdgeOnline page, select the [Business Builders] bullet.

4. Once you have arrived at the Edge Business Builders page, scroll down to the Small Business Practices section and click on <u>Develop and use a business plan</u>.

5. On the Small Business Practices page, scroll down to Describe your products/services and how they are produced.

Take this simple test

http://www.pawluk.com/pages/mktg/marketing_guerrillaj.htm

Ad/Vantage Pawluk
http://www.pawluk.com/indexj.htm

Hal Pawluk provides marketing advice to companies launching new products on his Ad/Vantage Web page, including a test for you to gauge how well your product will be accepted by consumers.

To try Hal Pawluk's test, do the following:

1. Type http://www.pawluk.com/indexj.htm in your Web browser's address box and press Enter.

2. On the Pawluk home page, scroll down and click on <u>Gorilla Marketing works better</u> under the Marketing Papers heading.

3. Once you reach the next page, scroll down to the bottom and click on <u>Gorilla paper</u>.

4. On the Gorilla marketing page, scroll down and locate Take this simple test.

Competing products and services

One thing you will want to do is to review how the competition highlights their product and service benefits. Look at some of the words (in bold) the following companies use in their advertising to describe their products and services.

Poland Spring
http://auburn.maine.com/tse/poland-me/psbco/welcome.html

Welcome to the great taste of Poland Spring, the northeast's favorite bottled natural spring water....**fresh, remarkable pleasing** spring water.

Cadillac
http://www.cadillac.com/cgi-bin/home.pl?sr

You have high expectations. That's why Cadillac has **higher standards**. To fulfill your aspirations, we've created four models of excellence. Seville exemplifies the perfect blend of technology, style, and performance. Eldorado embodies **freedom**, a responsive car for the spirited individual. DeVille commands **power and agility** for those who command quality. And Catera demonstrates just how **fun** a luxury car can be.

Mr. Coffee
http://www.mrcoffeeconcepts.com/office/mcc120.htm

Swing-out one piece brew basket. Reservoir opens wide for **easy pouring**. Easy-to-read fill marks inside the reservoir. Graduated water window. Two thermal fuses to guard against overheating. Warmer plate to keep coffee at **perfect temperature**. Compact size requiring **minimal counter space**. UL Listed commercial coffeemaker.

Nexxus
http://www.nexxushair.com/MAIN.HTM

Nexxus: Join us on a journey that leads to **beautiful** hair.

To see the benefits of your competitors' products and services, use one or more of the Web portal search engines, such as www.yahoo.com or www.excite.com. In the search box, try entering either the name brand of the competing product or the name of manufacturer.

Innovation...the key to success
http://www.rimart.com/innsucc.html

Ideas Exchange
http://www.rimart.com

The Ideas Exchange Web site "offers articles on inventions, patents, and licensing as well as expert resource directories." Its mission is to give your product the edge over the competition by using innovative and creative tools. For an informative article on innovation, try "Innovation...the Key to Success" contained on this Web site.

To view the article, do the following:

1. Type http://www.rimart.com in your Web browser's address box and press Enter.

2. Scroll down the page and click on Innovation...the Key to Success

What is a patent?

http://128.109.179.23/access/search-adv.html

U.S. Patent and Trademark Office

http://www1.uspto.gov

The U.S. Patent and Trademark Office (PTO) gives inventors "the exclusive right to their respective discoveries" for a period of 20 years. Since 1836, the PTO has issued more that 5.5 million patents. Information on all patents granted since 1976 can be found on the PTO Web site.

For instance, if you were planning to introduce a new golf club, you could search the PTO site for all golf club-related patents. From this search, you would find that 2,938 patents for golf clubs have been granted since 1976. This includes everything from RE35,596 Locking molded golf club headcover to 4,515,402 Golf ball retriever.

To access the search engine of the U.S. Patent Office, do the following:

1. Type http://www1.uspto.gov in the your Web browser's address box and press Enter.
2. On the USPTO home page, click on <u>Search</u> at the bottom of the page.
3. After you reach the Searching on the PTO Web Server page, select <u>Patent Data</u>.
4. Scroll down the page and select <u>Advanced Searches</u>, under the US Patent Bibliographic Database heading.
5. You are now on the U.S. Patent Advanced Search Page, and can submit a Query to find information about patents granted between 1976 and 1998.

Additional product and service resources

Shown here are some additional Web resources that might help you uncover product and service benefits:

DaVinci's Inventor Homepage!

http://sulcus.berkeley.edu/Invention

This Web site provides a list of useful resources for inventors and entrepreneurs.

Chemical Patents Plus

http://casweb.cas.org/chempatplus

This Web site allows you to search for specialized patent information, including titles and abstracts, for free. However, if you want to see the complete text or images, you will be charged a fee.

MicroPatent
http://www.micropat.com

Through MicroPatents search engines, PatentWEB and TrademarkWEB can assist you in assessing competitive information or conducting a trademark search.

Thomson & Thomson
http://www.thomson-thomson.com

Provides trademark and copyright services so that you can distinguish your products and services and safeguard them from consumer confusion.

IBM
http://patent.womplex.ibm.com/

This site allows you to search more than 2 million patents that were registered since 1971.

Chapter 17

Purchasing a Franchise

Imagine you are driving across the country for a summer vacation. It's lunchtime, and you have two hungry children in the backseat. You spot a sign on the highway and it says that both McDonald's and Billy Bob's Burgers can be found at the next exit. Which one do you choose? You would select Billy Bob's if you knew that its burgers tasted better and cost less than McDonald's. However, because you have never heard of Billy Bob's, you select McDonald's for its reliable service, quality, and pricing.

Because of the risk and amount of work involved in starting a new business, many entrepreneurs choose instead to purchase a franchise. Franchise-owned businesses enjoy a higher success rate than many independently owned businesses, because they provide established products and services accompanied by technical and managerial support.

However, there are trade-offs in selecting a franchise. You must follow the standard operating procedures established by the franchisor, and you will have little input in the marketing and product strategy.

This chapter provides descriptions of Web sites related to purchasing a franchise.

Self Test #1: Determine if you are suited to franchise ownership

http://www.franinfo.com/selftst1/default.html

FranInfo

http://www.franinfo.com/

The FranInfo Web site provides a wealth of information on franchising. In fact, the site's purpose is "to provide you with as much information regarding all aspects of franchising as we can within certain limits which constrain all commercial endeavors."

The FranInfo site has plenty of informative articles about franchising, including, "Why Buy a Franchise?" "History of Franchising," "How to Select the Right Franchise," a couple of self-tests, and "Franchises Most Frequently

Inquired About." If you are considering a franchise, then you should start with the Self Test #1: Determine if you are suited to franchise ownership.

To take the Self Test, do the following:

1. Type http://www.franinfo.com in your browser's address box and press Enter.
2. On the FranInfo home page, scroll down and click on Self Test #1 - Determine if you are suited to franchise ownership.
3. Then follow the onscreen instructions.

Franchises most frequently inquired about

http://www.franinfo.com/inquire.html

FranInfo
http://www.franinfo.com/

Another part of the FranInfo Web site that is worth a visit is "Franchises Most Frequently Inquired About." Here you will find "names and telephone numbers for a number of franchises which visitors to this website frequently request information on." Although this list includes such household names as McDonald's and Dunkin Donuts, it goes on to point out that many of these large franchises are sold out in the U.S.

To look at this list of "Franchises Most Frequently Inquired About," do the following:

1. Type http://www.franinfo.com in your browser's address box and press Enter.
2. On the FranInfo home page, scroll down and click on Franchises Most Frequently Inquired About.
3. A complete list of the largest franchises with phone numbers (toll-free numbers in many cases) is provided on this page.

Franchise UPDATE library

http://www.franchise-update.com/libr.htm

Franchise UPDATE Publications
http://www.franchise-update.com

Franchise UPDATE Publications covers the franchise trade, investment activity, and management through a series of newsletters, trade magazines, and directories. On its Web site, Franchise UPDATE allows you to explore the "Executives' Guide to Franchise Opportunities On-Line," "The Business Resale Network," "The Directory of Franchise Attorneys," and the "Franchise UPDATE Library."

The "Franchise UPDATE Library" includes a series of articles and checklists for the first-time franchise buyer. One checklist that you should review is the "Checklist to Evaluate a Franchisor." This page will familiarize you with many of the important questions you should ask prior to signing an agreement with a franchisor.

To review the "Checklist to Evaluate a Franchisor," do the following:

1. In your browser's address box, type http://www.franchise-update.com/libr.htm and press Enter.

2. On the Franchise UPDATE On-Line Library page, scroll down and click on <u>Checklist to Evaluate a Franchisor</u> under the Information for the First Time Franchise Buyer heading.

The executives' guide to franchise opportunities

http://www.franchise-update.com/exec.htm

Franchise UPDATE Publications
http://www.franchise-update.com

The "Executives' Guide to Franchise Opportunities," also available online from Franchise UPDATE, includes a brief but useful description of many popular franchises. For instance, the listings show:

- Date Established
- Company-Owned Units
- Franchised Units
- Total Investment Required
- Franchise Fee
- Royalty Percentage
- Advertising Percentage
- Contract Period(s)
- Expansion Plans
- Franchisee Qualifications
- Franchisor Special Features

To access the guide, do the following:

1. Type http://www.franchise-update.com in your Web browser's address box and press Enter.

2. Scroll down and click on The Executives' Guide to Franchise Opportunities On-Line.

3. On the Executives' Guide page, scroll down and select from the list of franchise companies actively expanding throughout the United States.

Business opportunity 500

http://www.entrepreneurmag.com/resource/bizop.hts

Entrepreneur Magazine
http://www.entrepreneurmag.com

This Web site contains multiple franchise databases. For instance, you can examine a listing of "New Franchises," the "Fastest Growing Franchises," or "Low Investment Franchises." In addition to these traditional franchise listings, you may also want to examine the "Business Opportunity 500" contained on this site.

According to Entrepreneur Magazine, "A business opportunity is any opportunity that enables you to make money. Specifically, it refers to the sale of a product or service in which the seller promises buyers they will make a profit, that there is a market for the product or service, or that the seller will buy any unsold merchandise back from buyers." For instance, if you were considering becoming a Fuller Brush representative, you could find additional information in the "Business Opportunity 500."

To explore the "Business Opportunity 500," complete the following steps:

1. Type http://www.entrepreneurmag.com in your Web browser's address box and press Enter.
2. Scroll down the page and click on Business Opportunity 500 under the Entrepreneur's Databases heading.
3. This will take you to the Business Opportunity 500 database, where you can search by keyword, name of business, or product or service.
4. Click on Browse by name and you will get an alphabetical listing of the Business Opportunity 500.

Franchising's fine print

http://www.dtonline.com/ba/ba.htm

Deloitte & Touche LLP
http://www.dtonline.com

Deloitte & Touche, the accounting and auditing firm, provides a revealing article about what you should look out for before signing a franchise agreement. "Franchising's Fine Print" helps the entrepreneur "learn how to spot an unfair agreement before signing one."

To read this article, do the following:

1. Type http://www.dtonline.com/ba/ba.htm in your Web browser's address box and press Enter.
2. On the Business Advisor page, scroll down and select the Franchising's Fine Print for more information on franchise agreements.

State offices administering franchise disclosure laws

http://www.ftc.gov/bcp/franchise/netdiscl.htm

Federal Trade Commission

http://www.ftc.gov/

The Federal Trade Commission (FTC), responsible for the consumer protection laws, oversees the marketplace "to eliminate acts or practices that are unfair or deceptive." On its Web site, the FTC has identified the 15 states that have franchise investment laws.

The franchise investment laws, designed to protect the potential purchaser, require the franchisor to give a presale disclosure, or "offering circular." These laws give you important legal rights, including the right to bring private lawsuits against the franchisor for violating the state disclosure requirements.

For additional information, and the list of states that have franchise investment laws, do the following:

1. Type http://www.ftc.gov/bcp/franchise/netdiscl.htm in your Web browsers address box and press Enter.

American Bar Association's forum on franchising

http://www.abanet.org/forums/franchising/

American Bar Association (ABA)

http://www.abanet.org

Within the American Bar Association, there is a forum with nearly 2,500 members that represents the field of franchise law. "The mission of the Forum is to be a center of information on laws affecting franchising, studying and investigating developments in the field, educating and providing a forum to promote improvements in the law as it affects franchising."

To locate the "ABA Forum on Franchising," do the following:

1. Type http://www.abanet.org/forums/franchising/ in your Web browser's address box and press Enter.

Additional franchise resources

The following are additional resources you may find useful.

International Herald Tribune

http://www.franchiseintl.com

From Argentina to Zimbabwe, the newspaper publishes a guide of major franchisors that are expanding overseas.

Franchise Handbook: On-Line
http://www.franchise1.com/articles/newsbyte.html

"News Bytes: What's Happening in the World of Franchising" reports on "topics that are of interest to everyone involved in franchising."

Access Franchise Directory Online
http://www.entremkt.com/access/gbreg.htm

EntreMKT provides a directory of more than 2,700 franchise organizations that can be searched by category, alphabetically, or by the investment required.

Income Opportunities Online
http://www.incomeops.com/online/franchops/franchops.html

Delivers informative articles and classified advertising on franchising, multilevel marketing, home-based opportunities, and import/export through its Web site.

Federal Trade Commission (FTC)
http://www.ftc.gov/bcp/conline/pubs/invest/buyfran.htm

For a complete discussion on the risks of purchasing a franchise, see the FTC article "A Consumer Guide to Buying a Franchise."

Chapter 18

Growth
Opportunity

Suppose you need to achieve sales of $1 million per year for your business to become profitable in the next three years. How would your business plan convince potential investors that your projected growth rate is achievable? If, after the first year, your plan showed sales of $300 thousand per year, then your business would need to achieve an annual sales growth rate of almost 60 percent per year to reach the $1 million per-year objective.

According to *Business Week's* list of "Hot Growth Companies" for 1997, this would put your business right in the middle the pack, because the average annual sales growth for these companies was 57.2 percent for the past three years. At the top of the list was Yurie Systems, a maker of telecommunications equipment, with a whopping 385.1 percent annual growth rate in sales.

One of the key statistics that will interest potential investors is the annual growth rate of your chosen business or industry. The growth rate is important because new businesses have a better chance of succeeding in an industry that is growing rapidly rather than one that is only growing moderately or not at all.

This chapter reviews Web sites that provide growth statistics for new markets.

Business Week's hot growth companies

http://www.businessweek.com/search.htm

Business Week Magazine
http://www.businessweek.com

This Web site has a searchable archive that dates back to January 1991. With its search engine, you can browse by cover image or issue date to locate a specific issue of the magazine. One that will be of interest to you is the May issue, titled "Hot Growth Companies."

"Hot Growth Companies" is a list of the 100 fastest-growing small companies. These businesses, which can have sales growth in excess of 200 percent per year, are ranked by sales, earnings, market value, and profitability.

To browse "Hot Growth Companies," follow these steps:

1. In your browser's address box, type http://www.businessweek.com and press Enter.
2. Next click on the [Archives] box located at the top of the page to start searching back issues of the magazine.
3. On the Search back issues page, scroll down to the Browse heading.
4. Select the May issues, for example the 05/05/97 - 06/23/97 choice.
5. After the Browse Back Issues page appears, locate and click on the Hot Growth Companies issue.
6. Scroll down to the Cover Story section, and select the TABLE: The Tops in Sales and Sales Growth.

Inc. 500 fastest-growing private companies

http://www.inc.com/500/

Inc. Magazine
http://www.inc.com

The magazine provides "advice, case studies, and big-picture overviews on the state of small business in the U.S." The Inc. 500, the magazine's annual list of the fastest-growing private companies in America, is another good source for growth rates. The Inc. 500 includes a business breakdown by five-year sales growth, latest annual revenues, and the type of business.

To browse the Inc. 500, do the following:

1. In your browser's address box, type http://www.inc.com and press Enter.
2. On the Inc. home page, locate and click on the [The Inc. 500] box.
3. Select the 1997 Inc. 500 list, or most current year for which it is available.
4. Choose view the entire 1997 list.

The 200 best small companies in America

http://www.forbes.com/forbes/97/1103/6010128a.htm

Forbes Magazine
http://www.forbes.com

"The Forbes Digital Tool," the Web site produced by the magazine, has its own perspective on the latest news, insights, and marketplace strategies. Every year the magazine publishes "The 200 Best Small Companies in

America," which is a great resource for exploring actual and potential growth rates. The list is very comprehensive and is broken down into categories that include an index by company name, ranking by return on equity, ranking by sales, ranking by profits, and ranking by market value.

To browse the magazine's list of "The 200 Best Small Companies in America" follow these steps:

1. In your browser's address box, type http://www.forbes.com and press Enter.
2. On the Forbes home page, locate and click on Current and back issues of Forbes magazine.
3. Select past issues or most current year for which it is available.
4. Locate the November issue, which includes The 200 Best Small Companies.
5. You can then select from a variety of articles and information on some of the best small companies in America.

Hottest 100 new small businesses

http://www.entrepreneurmag.com/resource/hot100.hts

Entrepreneur Magazine
http://www.entrepreneurmag.com

The magazine bills itself as "The Online Small Business Authority." This Web site has a multitude of special features, including "Entrepreneur Magazine Online," "Business Start-Ups Online," "10 Booming Homebased Businesses," "10 Top Businesses For 1998," and the "Business Resale Network."

The magazine and Dun & Bradstreet also publish the "Hot 100" on this Web site. This list of the hottest new small businesses is selected using the D&B database of business information and the following criteria: The owner must be active; the business must have been started in the last four years; and annual sales must exceed $1 million.

To browse the "Hot 100," do the following:

1. Type http://www.entrepreneurmag.com in your Web browser's address box and press Enter.
2. Locate and select Hot 100
3. You can then browse by rank, by 1997 sales figures, by industry type, or by state.

Fortune 500 largest companies in the U.S.

http://pathfinder.com/fortune/fortune500/

Fortune Magazine
http://pathfinder.com/fortune/

The "Fortune 500," published by the magazine, lists the largest companies in the United States. For instance, in 1997, the number-one company on the list was General Motors with $168 billion in sales. All of the company reports provide year-over-year sales and profit growth.

In addition to information on individual companies, you may also want to view the industry median data available through the Fortune Web site. This includes Changes in Revenues, Revenues per Employee, Revenues per Dollar of Equity, Changes in Profits, Total Return to Investors, Return on Equity, and more.

To review the "Fortune 500," complete the following steps:

1. Type http://pathfinder.com/fortune/ in your Web browser's address box and press Enter.
2. Scroll down the page and click on Fortune 500.
3. Once you are on the Fortune 500 page, you can select The Fortune 500 List for detailed reports on individual companies.

Key industrial and services clusters

http://www.ita.doc.gov/ita_home/itakeyin.html

International Trade Administration
http://www.ita.doc.gov

The International Trade Administration (ITA), which is part of the U.S. Department of Commerce, also provides "coverage of key industrial and services clusters: Technology and Aerospace, Tourism, Basic Industries, Environmental Technologies, Service Industries and Finance, and Textiles-Apparel and Consumer Goods."

To review some of the ITA data, perform the following:

1. In your browser's address box, type http://www.ita.doc.gov and press Enter.
2. On the ITA home page, locate and click on the [Industries] button.
3. You will then be brought to the page that lists the industry sectors.
4. Scroll down the page and find the industry that is applicable to your business.
5. For instance, choose CONSUMER GOODS.
6. On the Office of Consumer Goods page, select Industry Information.
7. From this page you will now have the opportunity to review multiple Web pages relating to the consumer goods industry.

Outlook trends tables

http://www.ita.doc.gov/industry/otea/usito98/tables.htm

International Trade Administration
http://www.ita.doc.gov

As part of the International Trade Administration, the Office of Trade and Economic Analysis (OTEA) publishes "Industry Sector Data." This data includes statistics for more than 100 manufacturing groups and products by SIC code. In addition to employment, wages and capital expenditures by industry, it also provides the year-over-year percentage growth in shipments.

To review these tables, do the following:

1. Type http://www.ita.doc.gov
2. On the ITA home page, scroll down an click on the [Trade Statistics] button.
3. This will take you to the Office of Trade and Economic Analysis.
4. Once you reach this page, scroll down and click on U.S. Industry Sector Data.

Economic forecasts

http://www.dismal.com/regions/regions.stm

Dismal Scientist
http://www.dismal.com

The Dismal Scientist, referring to an economist who predicted that the world would run out of food, provides considerable data on the economy. The Dismal Scientist Web site "provides forecasts on many different economic points to help improve your business decision-making." In addition to the national indicators, such as the producer price index and housing starts, this site also has regional economic data.

The regional data is available by 50 states, by 257 metro areas, or zip code. For instance, if you wanted to find out how fast Columbus, Ohio, is growing, try the following:

1. Type http://www.dismal.com in your Web browser's address box and press Enter.
2. Once you reach the Dismal Scientist home page, click on the [Data] button.
3. On the Dismal Data page, scroll down and select Regional Data.
4. After you reach the Regions page, select 257 Metro Areas.
5. From the Regional Economics page, scroll down the page and click on Columbus OH MSA.
6. You will then be able to see population density, the net population migration (whether people are moving in or out of the area), the unemployment rate, and personal income for Columbus.

Additional growth opportunity resources

Other sources that publish growth statistics for businesses include the following:

Upside
http://www.upside.com/texis/mvm/250

This magazine, a business technology publication, has its own ranking of businesses available through its Web site: "The Upside 250."

Fairmodel
http://fairmodel.econ.yale.edu

At this site, you can work with macroeconometric or multicountry econometric models for forecasting and policy analysis.

Worth Online
http://www.worth.com

For an opinion from a financial analyst about a specific company or industry, try entering the name in the Worth Online search engine.

Newspage
http://www.newspage.com

For current news on various industries, try Newspage. You can even create your own customized page to capture the latest news on your chosen industry.

The New York Times
http://www.nytimes.com

Try this newspaper's search engine to learn more about developments in your industry.

Biz Op, the Home Business Opportunity Center
http://www.bizopp.com/

Provides a listing of home-based businesses.

ResourceNet
http://www.c-store.com

Provides a synopsis of the monthly retail growth figures published by the U.S. Department of Commerce.

Chapter 19

Market Research

Suppose that you have decided to launch a new phone service for business customers. How would you find out if these customers are willing and able to buy your new service? You could simply start advertising and hope that some of the businesses bought your new service, or you could conduct market research to determine who the most likely purchasers would be. For instance, you might mail a survey to businesses in your area and ask them: Are they satisfied with their present service? Do they have a contract with another service provider? How much do they spend on phone service?

Once you have settled on an idea for starting a new business, it is necessary to conduct market research. Market research will increase your chances of success by identifying the target audience for the product, uncovering new market segments, highlighting the competition, and establishing the pricing for the product.

Market research comes in many forms, and you must select the most appropriate type based on your plan and resources. This chapter focuses on Web sites that provide advice on conducting primary market research.

Marketing research tips

http://www.busreslab.com/pasttips.htm

Business Research Lab
http://www.busreslab.com

A good place for some advice on conducting primary research is the Business Research Lab, which provides many useful articles on the subject, including:

- "Determining sample sizes for estimating proportions."
- "Eliminating leading questions."
- "Minimizing nonresponse in a mail survey."
- "Deciding how long mail questionnaires should be."
- "Sharing research expenses."

In addition to the general research tips and articles, the Business Research Lab provides a wealth of information on customer satisfaction, customer retention, employee satisfaction, internet surveys, and advertising.

To access the Business Research Lab, complete the following instructions:

1. In your browser's address box, type http://www.busreslab.com and press Enter.
2. On the Business Research Lab home page, click on the More Tips.
3. On the Marketing Research Tips page, scroll down and select the General Research Tips topic.
4. You will now be able to select from the articles mentioned above and many more.

Customer satisfaction surveys

http://www.busreslab.com/consult/sbcs.htm

Business Research Lab
http://www.busreslab.com

In addition to the research tips, the Business Research Lab also provides customer satisfaction surveys by industry type. Measuring customer satisfaction "can help you to maintain or gain competitive advantage by identifying areas for improvement." Surveys are available at a nominal fee for the following industries: apartments, new automobiles, auto service, used automobiles, bed and breakfasts, boutiques, home builders, grocery stores, hair salons, hotels, insurance claims, insurance (automobile), insurance (homeowner), mortgage companies, motels, real estate agencies, restaurants (long version), restaurants (short version).

For more information on the customer satisfaction surveys, do the following:

1. Type http://www.busreslab.com in your Web browser's address box and press Enter.
2. On the Business Research Lab home page, click on Small Business Solutions.
3. After you reach the Small Business Solutions page, click on Our Off-the-Shelf Surveys.
4. On the next page select Customer Satisfaction Surveys for Small Business.
5. This will take you to the Small Business Customer Satisfaction Page. Scroll down for the details on conducting surveys in your industry.

Inc. magazine archives

http://www.inc.com

This magazine's archives provide more than 5,000 online articles about "The State of Small Business—from 1988 to the present." These archives are another useful reference if you are planning to conduct market research. Some of the titles you might be interested in are:

On-the-cheap market research

http://www.inc.com/incmagazine/archives/06921081.html

> Author: Greco, Susan
> Issue: June 1992
> Summary: Uses libraries, knowledgeable CEOs, and university professors to gather inexpensive market research.

What's the best source of market research?

http://www.inc.com/incmagazine/archives/06921082.html

> Author: Greco, Susan
> Issue: June 1992
> Summary: Survey chart of the top sources of market research for new products.

Are you missing out on new markets?

http://www.inc.com/incmagazine/archives/10920301.html

> Author: *Inc.* Staff
> Issue: October 1992
> Summary: Chart on how effective market research is in finding new markets.

To access the magazine's archives, complete the following instructions:

1. In the browser's address box, type http://www.inc.com and press Enter.
2. On the Inc. Online home page, locate and click [*Inc.* magazine] button.
3. After you reach the *Inc.* magazine page, scroll down to the bottom of the page.
4. In the Select an Issue---> box, locate a June 1992 or October 1992 issue and press go (arrow).
5. On the next page all of the articles are listed. Move to the bottom of the page and select next.
6. Repeat this process until you reach the article.

How to write good survey questions

http://www.lodestone.com/tips/goodsur.htm

Lodestone Research
http://www.lodestone.com

Lodestone Research, L.L.C., is a full-service market research company that provides some useful tips on writing good survey questions. In market research "knowing how to write good survey questions is one of the best tools you can have!" Lodestone provides examples on how to pose questions, be exact, avoid ambiguity, avoid unwarranted assumptions, and avoid bias.

To access the Lodestone information, do the following:

1. In your browser's address box, type http://www.lodestone. com and press Enter.
2. On the Lodestone home page, click on the [Tips & Techniques] box.
3. After the Lodestone Tips & Techniques page appears, select the [Research Techniques] box in the lower left-hand corner.
4. Now you can select the How to Write Good Survey Questions.

Six ways to test your business idea

http://www.workingsolo.com/articles-news/Six-Ways-to-Test.html

Working Solo
http://www.workingsolo.com

Working Solo Online is for entrepreneurs and business owners. Through its Web site, you can read an article that provides general research tips, including:

- Looking through the yellow pages.
- Reading books and articles on the latest "hot" trends.
- Going to stores and see what other people are buying.
- Talking to friends and colleagues about your idea.
- Mailing a survey.

To read "Six Ways to Test Your Business Idea," do the following:

1. Type http://www.workingsolo.com in your Web browser's address box and press Enter.
2. On the Working Solo home page, click on the [Articles & News] button.
3. After you reach the Articles & News page, scroll down and click on Six Ways to Test Your Business Idea.

Sample size calculator

http://www.drgutah.com/calculator.html

Market Research Roundtable
http://www.drgutah.com/mrrc/mrrc.html

The Market Research Roundtable provides a comprehensive list of market research tools, including discussion groups to answer questions, industry news, and a directory. One tool you may want to try is the "Sample size calculator," which will indicate the range of error you can expect from your survey. This site also has many links to other sites through the "MRRC Research Site of the Month."

To find the Market Research Roundtable, do the following:

1. Type http://www.drgutah.com/mrrc/mrrc.html in your browser's address box and press Enter.
2. From the home page you will be able to select:
   ◆ Marketing Research Resources.
   ◆ Research Job Board / Marketing Research Roundtable.
   ◆ Sample Size Calculator / Downloadables.
   ◆ What is "Incidence?" / Research Co. Directory.
3. Select <u>Sample Size Calculator</u> to learn more about sample sizes.

Latest news from the research industry

http://www.worldopinion.com/newsstand.qry

WorldOpinion
http://www.worldopinion.com/home.qry

WorldOpinion, listed as the World's Market Research Web Site, provides more than 6,200 market research organizations from 95 countries. On this Web site, you will be able to access the latest news from the research industry, locate research findings, select links to newsletters and journals, and read a glossary of market research terms.

To review the Newsstand, complete the following steps:

1. Type http://www.worldopinion.com/home.qry in your Web browser's address box and press Enter.
2. Click on the [Newsstand] button.
3. On the Newsstand page, scroll down and click on <u>American Demographics</u>.

Additional market research resources

Here are a few additional Web sites that provide advice on primary market research:

Wilson Internet Services
http://www.wilsonweb.com/webmarket/mkt-research.htm

Although this site is mainly for Internet services, it does contain an interesting article on using the Web for primary market research. To find out more, read "Online Market Research Begins To Catch On."

Council of American Survey Research Organizations
http://www.casro.org

If you are looking for someone to conduct your market research, try the Council of American Survey Research Organizations (CASRO).

Princeton University Survey Research Center
http://www.princeton.edu/~abelson/index.html

If you're looking for additional market research outlets, try the Princeton site. It offers numerous links to other survey, research, and poll sites.

Market Research Center
http://www.asiresearch.com

This site is sponsored by ASI Market Research, an agency that offers television commercial advertising research and includes many links to the market research industry.

Gallup Organization
http://www.gallup.com

Although the Gallup Organization is famous for its polls on public opinion, it also covers many business-related issues. Try the Gallup archives available through its Web site.

SalesDoctors Magazine
http://salesdoctors.com/patients/1survey.htm

Proposes a six-step plan to create a survey that will help you to prospect for new customers.

Home Office Computing/Small Business Computing
http://www.smalloffice.com/guru/archive/mgresrce1.htm

This magazine provides many market-research-related items on its Web site, including a sample survey that you can use for your prospective customers.

Chapter 20 _____

Market
Segmentation

Is it less expensive to sell 10 cars that are painted black than to sell five that are painted black and five that are painted white? It depends! If the automobile buyer is indifferent to color, then it is less expensive to sell 10 black cars. If there are only a few buyers of black cars, because everybody prefers white, then it is less expensive to sell five white cars and five black cars.

Market segmentation is the process of dividing the market into sets of prospects that have similar needs or behavior patterns. Business owners need to identify their prospects, segment them into high-probability purchasers, and then convert them into customers.

Market segmentation starts by answering the following questions:

- Who are the customers or prospects?
- What are their unique characteristics?
- Why do they need these products and services?
- How many of them are there?
- How much do they spend on these products and services?

This chapter identifies Web sites that will help you to segment your market.

Product's positioning vital to getting noticed

http://www.amcity.com/denver/stories/111196/smallb6.html

American City Business Journals
http://www.amcity.com

American City Business Journals Inc. publishes a series of business newspapers that serve nearly 3.2 million readers in 37 metropolitan markets. Through its Web site, you will be able to access each newspaper's home page and obtain news and information about each American City market.

An article, titled "Product's Positioning Vital to Getting Noticed," stored in the American City Business Journals archives, defines a target market as "the group of people most likely to purchase your products. Your target market might be women skiers, men 25 to 54 who golf, or sales managers in Colorado in companies larger than 500 employees."

For a copy of the entire article, perform the following steps:

1. Type http://www.amcity.com in your Web browser's address box and press Enter.
2. On the American City Business Journals home page, type "target market" in the Back Issues box and click on Search.
3. Links for this article, along with many others on target marketing, will now appear on your screen.

In addition to the articles, you can actually use American City's search engine to get some information about a target market. For instance, if you wanted to learn about the pizza market in Atlanta, type "pizza and atlanta" in the Back Issues box and click on Search.

Buyer identification and behavior

http://www.toolkit.cch.com/Text/P03_2040.htm

SOHO Guidebook
http://www.toolkit.cch.com

The Small Office Home Office (SOHO) Guidebook Web site covers many aspects of business planning that are of interest to entrepreneuers and business owners, including starting your business, planning your business, getting financing for your business, marketing your product, office and equipment, people who work for you, managing your business finances, controlling your taxes, building your personal wealth, and getting out of your business.

Through its "Marketing Your Product" articles, the SOHO Guidebook explains the concept of how to target your market using segmentation. The article "Buyer Identification and Behavior" says, "The more exact the identification of your target buyer, the more efficient your marketing programs will be in generating sales from regular or heavy users."

For the entire article, do the following:

1. Type http://www.toolkit.cch.com in your Web browser's address box and press Enter.
2. On the SOHO Guidebook home page, click on Marketing Your Product.
3. Once you have reached the Marketing Your Product page, scroll down and select Analyzing the Market Environment.
4. On the Analyzing the Market Environment page, scroll down and select your target buyers for the complete article.

Tips to help you create a planning roadmap

http://www.dnb.com/planning/hplannin.htm

Dun & Bradstreet, Inc.
http://www.dnb.com

Dun & Bradstreet maintains a large database of business information to help its customers "make more profitable decisions." In addition to describing the services and information that D&B provides, its Web site also has a series of marketing-related articles that are of use to entrepreneurs and business owners. These articles include:

- "Harnessing the power of your customer information."
- "How to make the most of database marketing."
- "How to find hidden profits in your customer base."
- "How to target the right markets with direct mail."
- "Tips to help you create a business planning roadmap."

The article on "tips to help you create a business planning roadmap" describes key target marketing concepts such as market size and growth potential, customer value assessment, and customer value improvement.

To see this article, complete the following steps:

1. Type http://www.dnb.com in your Web browser's address box and press Enter.
2. On the D&B home page, click on Resource Center.
3. On the Resource Center page, use the drop down list and select Marketing.
4. After you reach the Marketing page, scroll down and click on Roadmap to Creating a Successful Business Plan for the entire list of tips.

Where to look for leads

http://www.morebusiness.com/running/marketing/v1n6.shtml

Business Resource Center
http://www.morebusiness.com

The Business Resource Center Web site is maintained by Khera Communications, a provider of Internet consulting and World Wide Web services. This site provides numerous articles about starting, marketing, financing, and managing a small business.

As you begin to settle on an approach for your target market, one of the things you will have to do is look for customer leads. The Business Resource

Center gives many of the traditional sources, such as referrals, trade shows, directories, and associations.

For the complete listing of lead sources, do the following:

1. Type http://www.morebusiness.com in your Web browser's address box and press Enter.
2. On the Business Resource Center home page, select <u>Marketing Department</u> from the Running Your Business heading.
3. Once you reach the Marketing Department page, click on <u>Where To Look For Leads</u>.

Ford's marketing goof

http://www.gmarketing.com/tactics/weekly_83.html

Guerilla Marketing Online
http://www.gmarketing.com

Guerilla Marketing Online, from the authors of the best-selling Guerilla Marketing series, is a "weekly Web magazine for small business, entrepreneurs, salespeople, and marketers of all kinds." Jay Conrad Levinson describes guerrilla marketing as achieving conventional goals, or success, with unconventional methods.

The Guerilla Marketing Web site has an excellent article about target marketing, titled "Ford's Marketing Goof." The article uses two examples, a failure and a success, taken from real-life stories at the Ford Motor Company. The story of the Edsel automobile was a failure because Ford did not use target marketing—the car was marketed to everyone. The Mustang, on the other hand, was a car that was designed for a very specific target audience—a first car for 20- to 30-year-olds, or a second car for 30- to 50-year-olds.

For this article on target marketing, do the following:

1. Type http://www.gmarketing.com in your Web browser's address box and press Enter.
2. On the Guerilla Marketing home page, select <u>Enter the web site now!</u>
3. In the Search the Site box, type "target marketing" and click on Find It!
4. You are then told that these key words were located in <u>GMO Tactics - The Weekly Guerrilla</u>.
5. Click on this selection

Current releases of regional and local labor statistics

http://www.bls.gov/regnhome.htm

U.S. Bureau of Labor Statistics
http://www.bls.gov

The Bureau of Labor Statistics (BLS), the "principal fact-finding agency for the Federal Government," provides a broad array of statistical information through its Web site, including data on industrial growth, productivity gains, employment, and the entire U.S. economy.

One of the statistics published by the BLS is the Consumer Price Index (CPI). The index, which provides an indication as to where prices are headed in general, takes into account numerous criteria that you may use to target your market. It considers consumer preference, income, population, and products and services available to consumers.

To see the CPI for a specific region, complete the following steps:

1. Type http://www.bls.gov in your browser's address box and press Enter.
2. Click on the [Regional Information] box for a map of the United States.
3. Select the region that is applicable for your business.
4. Once you reach the Region page, click on the [Regional Economy] box for the Consumer Price Index.

250 highest and lowest per capita incomes
http://www.bea.doc.gov/remd2/pcpirank.htm

Bureau of Economic Analysis
http://www.bea.doc.gov

The Bureau of Economic Analysis (BEA), an agency of the U.S. Department of Commerce, calls itself the "nation's economic accountant." On its Web site, the BEA ranks the "250 highest and lowest per capita incomes" of the 3,110 counties in the United States. For instance, in 1995, New York was ranked the highest on the list with $58,096 in average income, and Keya Paha, Nebraska, was the lowest with $5,956 in average income.

In addition to this listing, you can also find numerous other helpful segmentation tables, such as:

- Per capita personal income, by state and region, 1993-1997.
- Personal income, by state and region, 1993-97.
- Population, by state and region, 1993-97.
- Per capita personal income, by state and region, 1996-1997.
- Personal income, by component, state, and region, 1996-1997.
- Personal income and earnings, by major industry, state, and region, 1996-1997.
- Personal income, by state and region, 1997-1998.

To see the "250 highest and lowest per capita incomes," do the following:

1. Type http://www.bea.doc.gov in your Web browser's address box and press Enter.
2. Under the Regional heading, click on Data.
3. On the Regional Accounts Data page, click on highest and lowest in the State personal income section for a complete listing.

U.S. Gazetteer

http://www.census.gov/cgi-bin/gazetteer

U.S. Census Bureau

http://www.census.gov

The U.S. Census Bureau maintains a Web site containing demographic information on cities, states, and the entire nation. One page on the site that might help you with your target marketing is the U.S. Gazetteer. For instance, if your target market was a particular town in the United States, you could find the population using the ZIP code.

Below is an example of the information contained in the Gazetteer for the city of Madison, New Jersey.

Zip Code: 07940 PO Name: Madison (NJ)
Population (1990): 15,960
Location: 40.759939 N, 74.417868 W
Browse Tiger Map of area.
Lookup 1990 Census zipcode data from STF3B.

To use the Gazetteer, do the following:

1. Type http://www.census.gov in your Web browser's address box and press Enter.
2. On the Census Bureau home page, click on the [Search] box.
3. Once you have reached the Search the Census Bureau page, click on Place Search.
4. This will take you to the U.S. Gazetteer page, where you can simply enter the ZIP code to get the population for a requested town.

Additional market segmentation resources

The following are some additional resources that can help you with market segmentation:

American Demographics/Marketing Tools

http://www.demographics.com/index.html

Search through published articles, market research reports, and a newsletter of demographic trends and forecasts.

Investext Group
http://investext.com/Investext/content.shtml

This company "specializes in research and analyses of markets, companies, industries, products and geographic regions."

Database America
http://www.databaseamerica.com/html/index.htm

This company maintains a database of more than 11 million businesses and 165 million consumers that can be searched by SIC codes, type of business, geographic location, annual revenues, and number of employees.

STAT-USA
http://www.stat-usa.gov

A service provided by the U.S. Department of Commerce provides a multitude of economic indicators, including new housing starts, retail wholesale trade, per capita disposable income, personal income, wages and salaries by industry, manufacturing statistics, and much more. Try the Test Drive.

iMarket, Inc.
http://www.imarketinc.com

Helps you identify potential customers and provides information on more than 1,000 industries.

Home Office Computing/Small Business Computing
http://www.smalloffice.com/guru/mgspot2.htm

Created for today's entrepreneurs, this Web site combines business and technology advice on "how to start, run, and build a successful home-based business." Try the article "Increase your direct mail responses by learning the intricacies" to see how direct mailings make use of market segmentation.

Chapter 21

Competition

Many new companies are founded after an entrepreneur discovers a shortcoming with an existing product or service. For example, JCPenney did not like the pricing practices of many retail establishments at the beginning of the 20th century. People were charged prices based on what the retailer thought of them. JCPenney did not think this practice was fair, and decided to charge everyone the same price.

After the market has been segmented, and the research reveals that the proposed business can grow and become profitable, the next step is to study the competition. An analysis of the competition should include:

- Who is the competition?
- What features do their products and services offer?
- What benefits do they offer?
- How many competitors are there?

To help you find answers to these questions, this chapter reviews Web sites that provide advice on analyzing the competition.

Know your competition

http://www.entrepreneurmag.com/visa/visa_competition1.hts

Visa's SmallBiz Insider

http://www.entrepreneurmag.com/visa/

The Visa SmallBiz Insider, a collaboration between Visa and *Entrepreneur Magazine*, provides "timely tips and information designed to help you better manage and grow your business in an ever increasing competitive environment." One article appearing on this Web site, "Know Your Competition," discusses the importance of identifying your competitors and learning them inside and out.

For this article, and a list of "10 Questions Every Entrepreneur Should Answer," do the following:

1. Type http://www.entrepreneurmag.com/visa/visa_competition1.hts in your Web browser's address box and press Enter.

Competitive edge

http://www.entrepreneurmag.com/visa/visa_competition3.hts

Another article available through Visa's SmallBiz Insider, titled "The Competitive Edge," discusses how competition will actually spur your business to greater success.

For this article in its entirety, do the following:

1. Type http://www.entrepreneurmag.com/visa/visa_competition3.hts in your Web browsers address box and press Enter.

Checking out the competition

http://www.gohome.com/Sections/Marketing/199611-marketing2.html

Business@Home
http://www.gohome.com

Busisness@Home calls itself the "online gathering spot and information resource for the working-from-home community." Its Web site provides news and how-to information for home-based business owners, telecommuters, and corporate after-hours home workers.

"Checking out the competition," an article on the Business@Home Web site, suggests the following steps for analyzing your competition:

♦ Identify your competitors.
♦ Develop a list of required information.
♦ Gather the information.
♦ Build a competitive grid.
♦ Create your unique selling advantage.

To review the "Checking out the competition" article, perform the following actions:

1. Type http://www.gohome.com in your Web browser's address box and press Enter.
2. On the Business@Home home page, click on Marketing under the Sections heading.
3. Once you are on the Marketing page, scroll down to November 1996 for the article.

Outsmarting the competition

http://www.marketus.net/resources/tips/outsmart.html

Hamilton & Bond Advertising
http://www.marketus.net/index.html

Hamilton & Bond, an advertising agency specializing in strategic marketing planning, publicity, advertising, and inquiry management, offers some excellent advice for monitoring your competition. The article, "Outsmarting the Competition," available at this Web site, suggests you revisit the geography of your market, narrow your field of vision, monitor your inquiries, and more."

For a complete description of these tips and more, do the following:

1. Type http://www.marketus.net/index.html in your Web browser's address box and press Enter.
2. On the Hamilton & Bond home page, scroll down the page and click on the [Marketing and Business Resources] button.
3. On the next page, select Marketing Tips.
4. Once you are on the Tips to Use your Marketing Resources More Effectively page, click on Outsmarting the Competition.

Competitive intelligence success stories

http://www.fuld.com/success.htm

Fuld & Company, Inc.
http://www.fuld.com

According to Fuld & Company, a competitive intelligence (CI) consulting firm, "CI involves collecting and using public information about rival companies to make effective business decisions." You can keep tabs on your competitors by watching their job openings, new product announcements, and newsletters. The Fuld Web site has a list of success stories.

To access the Fuld & Company Web site, and to see the CI success stories, do the following:

1. Type http://www.fuld.com in your Web browser's address box and press Enter.
2. On the Fuld & Company home page, click on the [Resources/References] button.
3. On the Resources/References page, click on CI Success Stories.
4. Then follow the onscreen directions to find success stories in your line of business.

Survey on business intelligence in the U.S.

http://www.tfg.com/pubs/docs/O_EIII-97.html

Society of Competitive Intelligence Professionals
http://www.scip.org/homepage.html

The Society of Competitive Intelligence Professionals provides online forums and eletronic publications through its Web site. Although the site is mainly for competitive intelligence (CI) professionals, it includes some useful information about the CI process.

In an intelligence gathering article, the society explains that although there are many ways for you to gather information, some ways are more valuable than others. For instance, newspapers, trade press, and industry newsletters are the preferred methods, but the Internet, company employees, and suppliers are becoming very popular sources.

To see more about intelligence gathering, do the following:

1. Type http://www.scip.org/homepage.html in your Web browser's address box and press Enter.
2. On the SCIP home page, click on the [Surveys & Data] button.
3. On the Surveys & Data Menu page, select Survey on Business Intelligence in U.S. for the entire article.

Additional competition resources

Explore these other resources for more information.

Thomas Register of Manufacturers
http://www.thomasregister.com:8000

Try this site to locate competitors in a specific manufacturing industry.

Industry.Net
http://www.industry.net

Search through nearly 10 million products or 20,000 manufacturers and distributors to identify your competition.

Infotrade Online Services Tower
http://www.infotrade.co.uk/pubs/bookclub/books/book0137.htm

A synopsis of Michael E. Porter's book, *Competitive Advantage: Creating and Sustaining Superior Performance*, is available on this site.

IBM
http://ns.idm.ibm.com/insight/fore/roe1.html

This site provides a discussion on the competitive advantages that can be achieved with a direct sales force.

Dow Jones Business Directory
http://businessdirectory.dowjones.com

Evaluates business-related Web sites.

Chapter 22

Pricing

There is a common misconception among new business owners that profits lost because of lower prices will be made up through increased sales. Consider a $5 "Beanie Baby" that costs $4.50 to manufacture and nets 50¢ of profit on every sale. If the price is lowered to $4.75, or by 5 percent, then profits decline 25¢, or by 50 percent, on every sale! To make up for the loss in profit, the "Beanie Baby" manufacturer must increase sales by 100 percent, or sell twice as many as before just to maintain the same level of profitability.

One of the factors that has the greatest impact on business profitability is the price of the product or service. There is a tendency for business owners to set prices too low in order to boost unit sales. The price must be set in accordance with the quality, service levels, and perceived value of the product.

This chapter covers strategies that you can use when setting the prices for your products, including competitive position, pricing below competition, pricing above competition, and pricing for profitability.

Pricing tips

http://www6.americanexpress.com/smallbusiness/resources/starting/biz_plan/description/pricing.shtml

American Express Small Business Exchange
http://www6.americanexpress.com/smallbusiness

In addition to the Business Plan Workshop, the American Express Small Business Exchange Web site also provides some useful pricing advice through its pricing tips section. For instance, the site explains that you should "discuss what you will charge for your product or service and how you derived the price."

The site goes on to explain that "once you have briefly explained your pricing and rationale, discuss where this pricing strategy places you in the spectrum of the other providers of this product or service. Next, explain how your price will get the product or service accepted, maintain and hopefully increase your market share in the face of competition, and produce profits."

For all of the pricing tips from American Express, do the following:

1. Type http://www6.americanexpress.com/smallbusiness in your Web browser's address box and press Enter.
2. On the Small Business Exchange screen, click on the [Create a Business Plan] button.
3. Once you reach the Creating an Effective Business Plan page, scroll down and select Business Description.
4. On the Business Description page, click on Your pricing strategy for a complete list of pricing tips.

How to price your products and services

http://www.sba.gov/SCORE/ca/pricing.html

U.S. Small Business Administration
http://www.sbaonline.sba.gov

The Small Business Administration (SBA) reviews a wide variety of pricing strategies in "How to Price Your Products and Services" on its Web site. The SBA points out that many small businesses do not make a profit, because they fail to price their products and services correctly. "Before setting your prices, you must understand your product's market, distribution costs, and competition."

Potential pricing strategies recommended by the SBA:

◆ Retail cost and pricing.
◆ Competitive position.
◆ Pricing below competition.
◆ Pricing above the competition.
◆ Price lining.
◆ Multiple pricing.
◆ Service costs and pricing.

To review this article, do the following:

1. Type http://www.sba.gov/SCORE/ca/pricing.html in your Web browser's address box and press Enter.

Inc. magazine archives

http://www.inc.com

This magazine's archives provide more than 5,000 online articles about "The State of Small Business—from 1988 to the present." These archives provide another useful reference for pricing your products and services. Some of the titles you might be interested in are:

Benchmark: Make the price right

http://www.inc.com/incmagazine/archives/11960842.html

Author: *Inc.* Staff
Issue: November 1996
Summary: Some data showing how CEOs are finding price points for their new products and services.

Plan for profitable pricing

http://www.inc.com/incmagazine/archives/05951343.html

Author: Greco, Susan
Issue: May 1995
Summary: Authors of *The Strategy and Tactics of Pricing* (Prentice Hall, 1995) offer some advice about pricing.

Pricing gets easier

http://www.inc.com/incmagazine/archives/11931243.html

Author: Greco, Susan
Issue: November 1993
Summary: Results of survey asking how companies determined the price of their latest product or service.

You get what you pay for

http://www.inc.com/incmagazine/archives/10901551.html

Author: Brown, Paul B.
Issue: October 1990
Summary: Charging higher prices for customers who require more service.

Are your prices right?

http://www.inc.com/incmagazine/archives/01970881.html

Author: Greco, Susan
Issue: January 1997
Summary: An overview of how a revenue management pricing strategy can increase revenues without losing customers.

Pricing your service for profits

http://www.inc.com/incmagazine/archives/06921072.html

Author: Greco, Susan
Issue: June 1992
Summary: Company analyzes its profitability and discovers that mistakes in pricing can be costly.

Naming your price

http://www.inc.com/incmagazine/archives/07920801.html

Author: Mondello, Michael D.
Issue: July 1992
Summary: Using imaginative pricing strategies to increase profit.

To access the magazine's archives, complete the following instructions:

1. In your browser's address box, type http://www.inc.com and press Enter.
2. On the Inc. Online home page, locate and click the [Inc. Magazine] box.
3. After you reach the Inc. magazine page, scroll down to the bottom of the page.
4. In the Select an Issue ---> box, use the drop-down boxes to select the month and year of the issue and press go (arrow).
5. On the next page, all of the articles in the issue are listed. Move to the bottom of the page and select next.
6. Repeat this process until you reach the desired article.

Articles and case studies on pricing

http://www.entrepreneurmag.com/entre_search.hts

Entrepreneur Magazine Archives
http://www.entrepreneurmag.com

Entrepreneur Magazine Archives contain numerous articles and case studies on pricing. For instance, some of the titles contained on this Web site are:

- ◆ <u>Pricing Power</u>—How to strengthen your bottom line.
- ◆ <u>Priced To Sell</u>—Great idea, but can you profit from it? Here's how to find out.
- ◆ <u>Smooth Sailing</u>—Tips for improving cash flow.
- ◆ <u>Step 10: Set Your Price</u>—Find the right figure to make the highest profits.
- ◆ <u>Perfect Match</u>—Boost profits by matching the right customer with the right price.
- ◆ <u>Meg-A-Nut</u>—Case study of specialty nut store and its pricing strategy.

To find these articles and stories on pricing, do the following:

1. Type http://www.entrepreneurmag.com in your Web browser's address box and press Enter.
2. On the Entrepreneur Magazine home page, click on the [Search] box.
3. In the Keyword(s) text box, type in "pricing" and click on the [Search] box.
4. On the search results page, scroll through the articles and select from some of the titles listed here.

Additional pricing resources

In addition to the pricing resources already presented, there are a few others that you should explore. Some of these might include:

SOHO Guidebook

http://www.toolkit.cch.com/Text/P03_5000.stm

Try this site for some practical advice on packaging and pricing your product.

Small Business Advisor

http://www.isquare.com/existcust.htm

Provides advice on how your pricing strategy can be used to get your customers to buy more from your business.

EntrepreNet

http://www.enterprise.org/enet/library/pricing.html

Provides a complete discussion on pricing decisions, and how they can make or break your businesses.

Chapter 23

Advertising

In his book *Ogilvy on Advertising*, David Ogilvy tells readers, "Consumers still buy products whose advertising promises them value for money, beauty, nutrition, relief from suffering, social status, and so on. All over the world." The key for your advertising is to promise the consumer a benefit, as we discussed in a previous chapter, and then to deliver on the promise. If you promise consumers that your pizza tastes better, then they should agree with you after they consume their first slice.

You use advertising to position your new product in the target market identified by the segmentation analysis. To reach the target market, you must select the most appropriate form of advertising. The type of advertising you select will be based on the size of the market and the financial resources of your business and may include newspapers and magazines, yellow pages, radio, billboards, and television.

This chapter identifies Web sites that provide practical advice for creating advertising strategies.

Promotion, advertising, and public relations

http://www.toolkit.cch.com/Text/P03_7000.htm

SOHO Guidebook

http://www.toolkit.cch.com

The Small Office Home Office (SOHO) Guidebook Web site provides numerous articles on promotion, advertising, and public relations through its "Marketing Your Product" pages. Subjects that will be of interest to you include:

- ◆ Planning promotional programs.
- ◆ Promotion ideas.
- ◆ Advertising ideas.
- ◆ Public relations ideas.

For additional information on advertising from SOHO, do the following:

1. Type http://www.toolkit.cch.com in your Web browser's address box and press Enter.
2. On the SOHO Guidebook home page, click on Marketing Your Product.
3. After you reach the Marketing Your Product page, scroll down and select Promotion, advertising and PR for "the primary methods of communicating your message to your target customers."

Advertising ideas

http://www.toolkit.cch.com/Text/P03_7020.htm

Contained within the "Promotion, advertising and PR" pages of the SOHO Guidebook is a section called Advertising Ideas. This page points out that in order for advertising to be successful, it must be interruptive, credible, unique, and memorable. Additionally, there is an advertising checklist that will help you create memorable ads, and a discussion on the types of advertising used by small businesses.

For the entire SOHO article, do the following:

1. Type http://www.toolkit.cch.com in your Web browser's address box and press Enter.
2. On the SOHO Guidebook home page, click on <u>Marketing Your Product</u>.
3. After you reach the Marketing Your Product page, scroll down and select <u>Promotion, advertising and PR</u>.
4. Once you are on the promotion, advertising and PR screen, scroll down and click on <u>Advertising Ideas</u> that "discusses the use of advertising to inform, educate, persuade, and remind."

Advertising checklist

http://www.toolkit.cch.com/Text/P03_7030.htm

The SOHO Guidebook provides and eight-step checklist for your advertising, that includes the following tips:

♦ Make sure your ads are "on strategy" with your business positioning.
♦ Communicate a simple, single message.
♦ Stick with a likable style.
♦ Be credible.
♦ Ask for the sale.
♦ Make sure the ad is competitive.
♦ Make sure the ad looks professional.
♦ Be truthful.

For the eight-step advertising checklist from SOHO and a description of each item, do the following:

1. Type http://www.toolkit.cch.com in your Web browser's address box and press Enter.
2. On the SOHO Guidebook home page, click on Marketing Your Product.
3. After you reach the Marketing Your Product page, scroll down and select Promotion, advertising and PR.
4. Once you are on the Promotion, advertising and PR screen, scroll down and click on Advertising Ideas that "discusses the use of advertising to inform, educate, persuade, and remind."
5. From the Advertising Ideas page you can now select Our Advertising Checklist.

Advertising media

http://www.toolkit.cch.com/Text/P03_7031.htm

To see SOHO's list of advertising media, from print advertisements to direct mail, do the following:

1. Type http://www.toolkit.cch.com in your Web browser's address box and press Enter.
2. On the SOHO Guidebook home page, click on Marketing Your Product.
3. After you reach the Marketing Your Product page, scroll down and select Promotion, advertising and PR.
4. Once you are on the Promotion, advertising and PR screen, scroll down and click on Advertising Ideas that "discusses the use of advertising to inform, educate, persuade, and remind."
5. From the Advertising Ideas page you can now select Advertising Media.

An even dozen ideas to make your ads produce more results

http://salesdoctors.com/patients/1ad2.htm

SalesDoctors Magazine
http://salesdoctors.com

This magazine is produced electronically on the Web by SeaBird, a consulting firm that helps companies improve their sales results. This Web site has a wide variety of material on advertising, direct mail, networking, seminar selling, public relations, media, Internet lead generation, referral selling, and trade show marketing.

Some of the articles that might interest you include:

- ◆ "Building great ads."
- ◆ "High impact direct mail campaigns."
- ◆ "Warm calls beat cold calls any day."
- ◆ "An even dozen ideas to make your ads produce more results."

For instance, SalesDoctors suggests the following 12 steps for improving your advertising:

1. Add action to your headlines.
2. Tell the truth.
3. Talk like a real person.
4. Enhance the image.
5. Sow what you want to reap.
6. Tell customers what action to take.
7. Offer choices.
8. Make a small ad resemble a coupon.
9. Get professional design help.
10. Negotiate media pricing.
11. State the benefit.
12. Make one clear point.

For a complete explanation of these tips, do the following:

1. Type http://salesdoctors.com in your Web browser's address box and press Enter.
2. On the SalesDoctors home page, select SalesDoctors Archives.
3. After you reach the Archives page, click on the [Finding Patients—generating sales leads] box.
4. On the Finding Patients page, scroll down and select An even dozen ideas to make ads produce more.

The main reason I use classified ads

http://www.isquare.com

Small Business Advisor
http://www.isquare.com

The Small Business Advisor Web site, maintained by Information International, "is dedicated to advising and assisting individuals who are considering starting a business or who have already started a business." This site has a wide variety of information for small business, including some very informative pieces on advertising.

For instance, you can locate articles about "The Power of Classified Advertising," "How to Build Sales & Profits Fast With Simple Postcards," and

"How to Write Sales Letters That Sell Again and Again." Another article you should review is "The Main Reason I Use Classified Ads!" that explains how advertising should be used to stimulate further contact with your company, not to make a sale right away.

To see these informative articles on advertising, do the following:

1. Type http://www.isquare.com in your Web browser's address box and press Enter.
2. On The Small Business Advisor home page, select The Advisor under the Contents heading.
3. From the list of topics on the Advisor page, click on <u>Marketing</u>.
4. Scroll down the page under Marketing, and choose the <u>Why use Classified Advertising?</u> topic.

Successful promotion strategies

http://www.enterprise.org/enet/library/promote.html

EntrepreNet
http://www.enterprise.org/enet/

Entrepreneurs and business owners can find informative articles and useful links on EntrepreNet. For instance, you should read "Successful Promotion Strategies." In this article, EntrepreNet states that while promotion is an important element to create product awareness, it is usually not enough to generate sales. "Effective promotion must be implemented in conjunction with other marketing efforts that involve direct customer contact: telemarketing, direct mail, sales calls, and trade shows."

To locate "Successful Promotion Strategies" on the EntrepreNet Web site, do the following:

1. Type http://www.enterprise.org/enet/ in your Web browser's address box and press Enter.
2. On the EntrepreNet home page, click on [Library].
3. After you reach the Library page, scroll down and select <u>Elements of a Successful Promotional Strategy</u>.

What is meaningful content?

http://www.entreworld.org/DataEW/Traffic/RYB/RYBDefault.dbm

EntreWorld
http://www.entreworld.org/

EntreWorld sorts and lists the best resources available on the Web for entreprenuers. For instance, if you are interested in information on advertising, you might get a list of articles such as the following:

- ◆ "Copywriting basics."
- ◆ "The 10 most expensive yellow pages advertising mistakes."
- ◆ "10 ways to stretch your advertising budget."
- ◆ "Catalog marketer: creating, producing, and mailing profitable catalogs."
- ◆ "Danger—comparative advertising."

To read this site for advertising-related material, do the following:

1. Type http://www.entreworld.org/ in your Web browser's address box and press Enter.
2. On the EntreWorld home page, click on the [Growing Your Business] button.
3. On the Growing Your Business page, click on <u>Advertising</u> under the Marketing & Sales heading.
4. You will now be presented with a list of advertising-related articles, such as those mentioned here.

Additional advertising resources

The following are several additional resources that you may want to review prior to finalizing your advertising strategy.

Advertising Age
http://www.adage.com

This magazine has been in print for more than 65 years, and its associated Web site is an excellent source for marketing and advertising news.

Advertising Law Internet Site
http://www.webcom.com/~lewrose/home.html

This site is maintained by the law firm of Arent Fox, and contains a law library on such topics as customer lists, telemarketing, ad substantiation, product demonstrations, and unsolicited faxing.

Idea Café
http://www.ideacafe.com/bizcomm/bczremember980316.html

A Web site designed for the entrepreneur that provides some interesting advertising tips, such as "Newsletter Design—Don't Sweat It!"

Entrepreneur's Mind
http://www.benlore.com

Produced by the Benlore Company, this Web site has plenty of advice on advertising from successful entrepreneurs.

Chapter 24

Location

Have you ever noticed that video rental stores tend to be situated near grocery stores? In fact, many grocery stores even have their own video rental department. Video store owners have discovered that placing their outlets near high-traffic locations, especially grocery stores, is beneficial to their rental business. But more importantly, consumers find it convenient to rent and return tapes near a location that they must frequent anyway.

The site location can be critical to the success or failure of your proposed business. You should take into consideration customer needs, accessibility to both suppliers and customers, and security arrangements. Questions you must answer when considering a location include:

- What is the address?
- Does it meet the space requirements?
- How does this location compare to others?
- What types of delivery services are available?
- Does the local zoning permit this type of business?

This chapter covers Web sites that are dedicated to helping you select the best location for your business.

Store location: "Little things" mean a lot

http://cbsc.org/sask/bis/5778.html

Canada Business Service Centre

http://www.cbsc.org

The Canada-Saskatchewan Business Service Centre "was established to provide businesspeople with a single access point for information that may be spread across many government departments and agencies, or located in a variety of other places." In addition to providing lists of manufacturers, suppliers, and associations, the Business Service Centre also has an extensive library of informative articles for small businesses.

One article, called "Store Location: 'Little Things' Mean A Lot," should be of interest if you are planning to open a retail or convenience store. Because store location may lead to the success or failure of your business, it is important that you consider compatibility and zoning as part of your selection criteria.

To view this article on selecting a location site, do the following:

1. In your Web browser's address box, type http://cbsc.org/sask/bis/5778.html and press Enter.

How to: Find the perfect location

http://www.entrepreneurmag.com/page.hts?N=5794&Ad=S

Business Start-Ups Online
http://www.entrepreneurmag.com

Business Start-Ups Online, an *Entrepreneur Magazine* publication, has a few articles on site selection, including "How To: Find The Perfect Location." In this article, the author describes "six factors to consider before setting your site," as follows:

1. Traffic patterns.
2. Where your customers are located.
3. How much the space will cost your business.
4. Where your suppliers are located.
5. How close the business is to public transportation.
6. Where your employees live.

To see this article and a few others on selecting a location, do the following:

1. Type http://www.entrepreneurmag.com in your Web browser's address box and press Enter.
2. On the Entreprenuer Magazine home page, scroll down and click on Business Start-Ups Magazine.
3. After you reach the Business Start-Ups Online page, locate Search Business Start-Ups Magazine.
4. In the Keyword(s) box, type Location. Also make sure you select All Issues and All Months in the appropriate drop-down boxes. The Areas to search box should say Business Start-Ups. Then click on the [Go] box.
5. At the conclusion of the search, you should be able to select the article <u>How To: Find The Perfect Location</u>.

Saturation analysis

http://www.c-store.com/newpage14.htm

Convenience.Net
http://www.c-store.com/

The Convenience.Net Web site provides information, articles, and research trends for the convenience store industry. For instance, a saturarion study contained on this site explains that the total population of a geographic area divided by the number of convenience stores should be around 3,000. If it falls below 1,000, expect stores to close. If it rises above 5,000 expect new stores to open.

For the entire Saturation Analysis article, do the following:

1. Type http://www.c-store.com in your Web browser's address box and press Enter.
2. On the ResourceNet home page, scroll down and select Trends/Reports.
3. After you reach the Trends/Reports page, click on the [Saturation] button.

New plant report

http://www.conway.com/cdi/dataserv/npsample.htm

SiteNet
http://www.sitenet.com

SiteNet, a Web site maintained by Conway Data, is devoted to the field of Geo-economics. This is a science that can be used to select the optimal location for headquarters offices, manufacturing plants, research centers, and distribution facilities, by considering the resources and manpower available in a geographic region.

The "New Plant Report," a research tool for executives, planners, and consultants, is available through SiteNet. The report contains more than 60,000 new plant expansion records that include location of the project, company name, product to be manufactured or service performed, SIC code, type of industry, stage of development, anticipated number of employees, square footage, amount of investment, and a contact name and telephone number.

To view the "New Plant Report," do the following:

1. In your Web browser's address box type http://www.sitenet.com and press Enter.
2. On the SiteNet home page, click on Conway Data, Inc.
3. After you reach the Conway Data Information page, select Pioneering in Geo-Economics.

4. On the Geo-Economics page, scroll down and locate bullet #4 under the heading Specific contributions of McKinley Conway.

5. Then click on <u>new plant reporting</u> for the entire document.

Site Selection Magazine/IDRC

http://www.sitenet.com/idrcnet/communicator/

International Development Research Council (IDRC)
http://www.sitenet.com/idrcnet/

Other areas of SiteNet that might interest you are The International Development Research Council (IDRC) and Site Selection Magazine. The magazine's mission is "to publish information for expansion-planning decision-makers," such as CEOs, facility planners, and corporate real estate executives. The IDRC is an association of real estate executives numbering 2,500 worldwide.

For more information from Site Selection Magazine or the IDRC, do the following:

1. Type http://www.sitenet.com in your Web browser's address box and press Enter.

2. Then you can choose either of these sections from the SiteNet home page.

Empowerment zones and economic communities

http://www.hud.gov/cpd/ezec/ezecsucc.html

U.S. Department of Housing and Urban Development
http://www.hud.gov/core.html

The U.S. Department of Housing and Urban Development (HUD) was created in 1965 "to help people create communities of opportunity." One of the business opportunities that might be of interest to you is the Empower-ment Zone and Enterprise Community program, which promotes economic activity in targeted communities. For instance, this Web site tells of a local Boston manufacturing company that broke ground with a $1.45 million Empowerment Zone and will have 70-plus employees by the end of the year!

For a list of success stories about Empowerment Zones, do the following:

1. Type http://www.hud.gov/core.html in your Web browser's address box and press Enter.

2. On the HUD home page, click on Business Opportunities.

3. Once you reach the Business Opportunities page, select Best Practices.

4. On the Best Practices page, click on EZ/EC best practices.

Geographic Names Information System (GNIS)

http://mapping.usgs.gov/www/gnis/

U.S. Geological Survey

http://www.usgs.gov

According to its Web site, "the U.S. Geological Survey (USGS) provides the nation with reliable, impartial information to describe and understand the Earth." Contained within the USGS, is the Geographic Names Information System (GNIS), which lists nearly 2 million physical and cultural geographic features of the United States. These features, which include buildings, bridges, churches, and rivers, are identified and located by state, county, and geographic coordinates.

For instance if you wanted to learn more about the buildings in your state, do the following:

1. In your Web browser's address box, type http://www.usgs.gov and press Enter.
2. On the U.S. Geological Survey home page, click on <u>Mapping</u> under the Science Topics heading.
3. Once you reach the National Mapping Information page, select <u>Geographic Names Information</u> (GNIS) under the Online Systems heading.
4. On the GNIS page, click on <u>United States and Territories</u> in the Query the GNIS Online Data Base table.
5. This will take you to the Geographic Names Information System Data Base Query Form.
6. Complete the form and select Send Query.

Environmental guidelines for the planning of projects

http://www.reinet.com/library/construction/file32.htm

Real Estate Information Network (REINET)

http://www.reinet.com

The Real Estate Information Network (REINET) is a general-purpose Web site covering the real estate industry. In addition to directories, a comparable transaction database, and classified advertising, REINET has a library with articles on selecting a location. For instance, "Environmental Guidelines for the Planning of Projects," recommends that a Phase I Environmental Audit be performed on the property during the planning phase. This would include reviewing:

♦ Asbestos and radon surveys
♦ Building department records

◆ Previous owner's records
◆ Courthouse records

To access REINET for the article on environmental considerations, do the following:

1. Type http://www.reinet.com in your Web browser's address box and press Enter.
2. On the REINET home page, click on Library.
3. Under the Articles, Special Services and Links to Other WEB Sites of the Library page, select Construction and Development.
4. On the next page, click on the story.

Find a mortgage

http://mortgagequotes.com/home.html

National Mortgage Rates—Date and time Stamped
http://www.microsurf.com

For the latest financing rates, try "The Largest Mortgage Database in Cyberspace from Microsurf." This Web site has more than 5,000 pages of constantly updated mortgage rates from lenders in every state.

For a mortgage financing rate in your state, do the following:

1. In your Web browser's address box, type http://www.microsurf.com and press Enter.
2. On the Microsurf home page, select the [Find a Mortgage] button.
3. On the next page, click on the [Select Today's Mortgage Rates In Your State] button.
4. This will take you to a map of the United States. Click on the state of your choice.
5. Once you reach Today's Mortgage Rates, you can select the type of loan that best meets your financing needs.

Switchboard directory

http://www.switchboard.com

Switchboard is an Internet directory service that provides 106 million residential listings and 11 million business listings nationwide. One feature that will be of use to you in selecting a location for your business is the "Business Category Search" by city and state.

For instance, if you wanted to locate all of the restaurants in your city, do the following:

1. Type http://www.switchboard.com in your Web browser's address box and press Enter.

2. On the Switchboard home page, click on the [Find Business] button.
3. After you arrive on the Business Category Search page, locate the drop-down list from #1 (Type Category). Pick a category from this list.
4. From the drop-down list select Restaurant, or your category of choice.
5. Scroll down to #3 and type the city and state for the locations.
6. Click on the [Search] box.
7. Once Switchboard locates all of the establishments, you can even get a map of their geographic location.

Define your community

http://www.comfind.com/search/comfind

ComFind
http://www.comfind.com

ComFind offers a business Web site directory. For instance, you could look up all of the Web sites in your community by phone number or city.

To use ComFind, do the following:

1. Type http://www.comfind.com in your Web browser's address box and press Enter.
2. Click on the [Search Local Web Sites] button.
3. Enter the phone number or city and state information you wish to search.

Additional location resources

The following are many additional resources that you might use in search of the perfect location for your business.

BigBook
http://www.bigbook.com

Locates addresses and phone numbers for more than 16 million businesses. Also includes a personal address book, maps, and a virtual city.

555-1212.com
http://www.555-1212.com

Another good source for telephone numbers, area code and country code information, e-mail addresses, and Web site locations.

WhoWhere
http://www.whowhere.com

Started in 1994, this site offers business URLs, e-mail addresses, and telephone directory listings.

www.REALTOR.com
http://www.realtors.com

Operated by RealSelect, Inc., this is the official Web site of the National Association of Realtors.

Commercial Real Estate Eastern United States Guide
http://www.com-re.com

A listing of commercial real estate for sale in the Eastern United States.

Real Estate Resources in the Southeast
http://www.realty-resources.com

Locates commercial properties for sale in the Southeast.

National Association of Industrial and Office Parks (NAIOP)
http://www.naiop.org

A trade association for developers, investors, owners, and asset managers of commercial real estate in the United States and Canada.

Macfadden Business Communications Group
http://www.csnews.com

A publisher serving the mass retail, food, and supermarket industries.

C-Store Central
http://www.cstorecentral.com

A Web site operated by the National Association of Convenience Stores that provides news and information on the convenience store industry.

Chapter 25

Management and Personnel

If you are fortunate enough to be starting a new business that does not require you to be the chief receptionist, head accountant, national account manager, and technical strategist all at the same time, then you will have to think about hiring some support. Most new businesses are big on ideas but short on resources, and must make hiring decisions very carefully.

People are the most valuable resource a business has and will ultimately determine the success or failure of the enterprise. It is important for you to conduct a personal skills assessment, and then hire people with complementary skills. For instance, a sales-oriented owner will need to hire people who specialize in the operations and administration of the business.

This chapter presents a number of Web sites that are devoted to personnel administration.

Entrepreneur's quiz

http://www.bizresource.com/smallbiz.htm#quiz

BizResource
http://www.bizresource.com

BizResource provides information and assistance to entrepreneurs and small business owners. This Web site contains the "Entrepreneur's Quiz," which will help you identify your strong business skills and those that need improving.

To take the "Entrepreneur's Quiz," do the following:

1. In your Web browser's address box, type
   http://www.bizresource.com and press Enter.
2. On the BizResource home page, click on the [Small Biz] box.
3. From the Small Biz page, click on the [Entrepreneur's Quiz] button to take the test.

HR Magazine

http://www.shrm.org/hrmagazine/

Society for Human Resource Management (SHRM)
http://www.shrm.org

The Society for Human Resource Management (SHRM) is an organization that represents more than 90,000 professionals and students worldwide. It provides information services, conferences, seminars, and publications for human resource professionals.

SHRM also publishes HR Magazine, which is available through its Web site. A recent issue included the following features:

- "Drugs in the workplace."
- "Employers learning to live with AIDS."
- "Recruitment agenda: Computer-assisted interviewing shortens hiring cycle."

The Web site also has a search engine that allows you to find past articles.

To see the latest issue, do the following:

1. In your Web browser's address box, type http://www.shrm.org and press Enter.
2. On the SHRM home page, scroll down and click on HR Magazine.
3. This will bring you to the Table of Contents for the latest issue.
4. To search for a specific article in back issues, scroll down the page and click on Search HR Magazine Online.

Compensation and benefit survey information
http://www.hronline.org/research/research.htm

Employers Group
http://www.hronline.org/index.html

The Employers Group is a nonprofit human resources management association with nearly 5,000 of California's private- and public-sector employers. Through this Web site you can obtain a wide variety of com-pensation and benefit survey information, including:

- Executive compensation survey
- Supervisory and management compensation survey
- Professional and technical compensation survey
- Information systems compensation survey

To see the compensation survey information, do the following:

1. Type http://www.hronline.org/index.html in your Web browser's address box and press Enter.

2. On the Employers Group home page, scroll down and select Research Department.

3. Then on the Compensation and Benefit Survey Information page, you can click on the <u>Professional and Technical Compensation Survey</u>.

Employee or contractor?

http://www.gohome.com/

Business@Home
http://www.gohome.com/

Busisness@Home, a resource for those working at home, explains some of the differences between hiring employees and contractors. Although it may be less expensive for you to hire an independent contractor, you must follow the IRS guidelines to determine employment status. According to Business@Home, "the issue boils down to one of control. If the business owner can control the person's work product, workplace, and work effort, then you are employing this person."

For the complete article, "Employee or contractor?" do the following:

1. Type http://www.gohome.com in your Web browser's address box and press Enter.

2. On the Business@Home page, click on <u>Finance & Taxes</u> under the Sections heading.

3. After you reach the Finance & Taxes page, click on the <u>Index</u>.

4. Scroll down to March 1997 and select the <u>Employee or contractor?</u> article.

Creating an ownership culture

http://www.fed.org/library/articles/ward.html

WestWard Pay Strategies
http://www.westwardpay.com

WestWard Pay Strategies, Inc., is a compensation consulting firm "specializing in strategic executive, sales, and other cash and stock-based incentive compensation matters for leading growth, technology, and other forward-thinking companies." The founders of this company have made many of their articles and studies available through the Web site.

For instance, "Creating An Ownership Culture" warns that simply giving employees shares of stock in your company does not create an ownership culture. To create an employee-run culture, you must:

♦ Share information.

♦ Teach employees new habits.

- Ask employees their opinion.
- Listen to employee's answers.
- Learn from employees and other companies.

For this entire article, perform the following steps:

1. Type http://www.westwardpay.com in your Web browser's address box and press Enter.
2. On the WestWard home page, click on Publications.
3. Scroll down the page and select the <u>Creating An Ownership Culture</u> article.

Your Christmas leadership message

http://www.smartbiz.com/sbs/news.htm

Smart Business Supersite (SBS)

http://www.smartbiz.com

The Smart Business Supersite (SBS) Web site provides plenty of "how-to" information, checklists, and reports for all types of businesses. SBS also has a series of articles on employee communications and performance management. For instance, "Your Christmas Leadership Message" explains that "Christmas is a great time to observe and begin to understand the true nature of your team and how work really gets done."

To see this article and others on SBS, do the following:

1. In your Web browser's address box, type http://www.smartbiz.com and press Enter.
2. On the SBS home page, click on Daily News Briefs And Monthly Columnists.
3. On the Business News page, scroll down and select <u>Scott Arbuthnot On Performance Management Problem Solving</u> under the Columns heading.

Recruiting and retaining employees

http://www.adp.com/emergingbiz/tool/business/rre7.html

Automatic Data Processing

http://www.adp.com

Automatic Data Processing (ADP) provides payroll and payroll tax transaction processing services for business. The ADP Web site includes some informative articles on recruiting and retaining employees, including "Selecting and Managing Recruiters," "Human Resources Issues," and "Compensation—Cash vs. Non-Cash Compensation."

According to ADP, "If you are able to identify and hire a key employee quickly, the amount of money you spend on recruiting fees will be minimal in comparison to the ability to capitalize on new business opportunities with talented staff."

For a complete description on how to work with recruiters, do the following:

1. In your Web browser's address box, type http://www.adp.com and press Enter.
2. On the ADP home page, click on the [Visit Our New Emerging Business Center] box.
3. After you reach the Emerging Business Services page, select the [Business Tools] button.
4. On the Business Tools page, scroll down and click on Business Resource Center.
5. You can then select the article from the Business Resource Center page by clicking on Performance Evaluations.

Additional management and personnel resources

The following are more personnel-related Web sites that will help you find and retain the best employees.

AFL-CIO
http://www.aflcio.org/home.htm

The AFL-CIO is a labor union whose mission is "to improve the lives of working families and to bring economic justice to the workplace and social justice to the nation."

Disability Forum
http://www.eease.com/disability/

Sponsored by Fortis Benefits, the Disability Forum is a Web site for employees and employers to better understand disability.

workindex.com
http://www.workindex.com/workindex/

Created by Cornell University and *Human Resource Executive* magazine, this Web site has information for those interested in human resources, labor relations, staffing, leadership, recruiting, and motivation.

Business Research Lab
http://www.busreslab.com/sbemploy.htm

Employee satisfaction surveys are available on this site for a nominal fee.

Electronic Recruiting News
http://www.interbiznet.com/hrstart.html

A daily online newsletter for recruiters and human resource specialists.

Workforce Magazine
http://www.workforceonline.com

Provides advice for human resource executives and managers.

Center for the Study of Work Teams
http://www.workteams.unt.edu

Supports the development and implementation of collaborative work systems to improve organizational effectiveness.

Employee Relations Discussion Lists
http://www.mtsu.edu/~rlhannah/erlists.html

Provides many URLs of faculty and professionals specializing in employee relations.

Foundation for Enterprise Development (F.E.D.)
http://www.fed.org

A nonprofit organization that helps entrepreneurs and executives "use equity compensation towards greater growth and success."

Chapter 26

Training

Training has become such an important issue for business that many employers now require every employee to attend five or more training days per year. That can amount to a staggering 5 percent of the total time on the job in a given year. Employees are trained on everything from the latest computer system to answering the phone in a professional manner.

According to the American Society for Training and Development, "The most consistent advantage for business and for individual employees is the ability to learn faster and perform more efficiently than the competition.... Performance heads the list of critical issues for most companies today. The demand from the marketplace for speed, customization, timeliness, quality, and variety of products and services has changed the landscape for doing business. The use of technology and the relentless speed of change have changed the nature of work itself and the skills that working people need."

This chapter covers Web sites that provide additional information on improving the skills of employees to boost their performance.

Training industry trends

http://www.astd.org/virtual_community/community_trends/training_trends_t d1197.htm

American Society for Training and Development (ASTD)
http://www.astd.org/index.html

The American Society for Training and Development (ASTD) provides "leadership to individuals, organizations, and society to achieve work-related competence, performance, and fulfillment." A company can obtain a sustainable competitive advantage by learning faster and performing more efficiently than the competition. For ideas on how your company can beat the competition through training, read about some of the latest trends in the industry.

To access the ASTD Web site and find this article, do the following:

1. In your Web browser's address box, type
   http://www.astd.org/index.html and press Enter.

2. On the ASTD home page, click on the logo to move to the next page.
3. After you reach the Virtual Community page, select the [Find] box.
4. On the Find page, type "Training industry trends" in the Search Virtual Community box and click on [Search].
5. On the next page, click on <u>News and Trends Community</u> to locate the latest training developments.

Ranges of average training expenditure as a percentage of payroll

http://www.astd.org/virtual_community/comm_trends/98soi_slide_train_expenditures.html

In addition to training-related articles on its Web site, ASTD also provides some data that will be of interest to you as your prepare your training budget. For example, the Training Expenditure table shows that training costs are near 1.5 percent of payroll.

Other graphs and tables on this Web site, include:

♦ Percentage of Employees Trained.
♦ Training Time by Course Type.
♦ Training Dollars by Course Type.
♦ Staff and Sources.
♦ Outsourcing by Industry.
♦ Use of Delivery Methods.
♦ Training Time by Delivery Method.
♦ The Training-Performance Link.

To see a breakdown of average training expeditures, do the following:

1. In your Web browser's address box, type http://www.astd.org/index.html and press Enter.
2. On the ASTD home page, click on the logo to move to the next page.
3. After you reach the Virtual Community page, click on [Library].
4. On the Library page, scroll down and click on Training Statistics.
5. You can then select from any of the tables listed above.

Why should you train your workers?

http://www.ronkurtus.com/training/tipstraining.htm

Kurtus Technologies
http://www.ronkurtus.com/kurtech/default.htm

Kurtus Technologies, a company specializing in education and training, provides numerous articles on its Web site regarding the benefits of training, including, "Why Should You Train Your Workers?," "Why Should You

Train Your Customers?" and "What is the Best Delivery Medium to Use for Training?"

According to Kurtus, you should train your employees because "skilled workers increase profits." These employees work faster with fewer mistakes, and contribute to the bottom line through increased productivity. Your training should focus on particular skills, equipment, or products.

For this and other training-related articles from Kurtus, do the following:

1. Type http://www.ronkurtus.com/training/tipstraining.htm in your Web browsers address box and press Enter.
2. On the Tips on Using Training and Instruction page, select "Why Should You Train Your Workers?"

What is human performance technology?

http://www.ispi.org

International Society for Performance Improvement (ISPI)
http://www.ispi.org

The International Society for Performance Improvement (ISPI), founded in 1962, represents more than 10,000 members in the United States and Canada. "ISPI's mission is to improve the performance of individuals and organizations through the application of Human Performance Technology." This is a process that will help you identify the current abilities of your work force, the abilities required to accomplish your goals, and cost effective ways to fill any gaps between the current and required abilities of your work force.

For a complete description of Human Performance Technology, do the following:

1. In your Web browser's address box type http://www.ispi.org and press Enter.
2. On the ISPI home page, scroll down and click on What Is HPT? under the Professional Services heading.

What are the top five work values?

http://www.lorenet.com/Lorefyi/results.html

Lore International Institute (LORE)
http://www.lorenet.com

The Lore International Institute (LORE) delivers professional training and consulting to improve interpersonal, leadership, sales, and marketing skills. On its Web site, LORE identifies the top five work values as follows:

- Enjoyment
- Integrity

- ◆ Achievement
- ◆ Balance
- ◆ Knowledge

By knowing your employees' values, "you know what will draw their attention and capture their energy."

To see the "Top Five Work Values" on the LORE site, do the following:

1. In your Web browser's address box, type http://www.lorenet.com/Lorefyi/results.html and press Enter.

Training Technology Resource Center (TTRC)

http://www.ttrc.doleta.gov

One-Stop/LMI
http://www.ttrc.doleta.gov/onestop/

The Training Technology Resource Center (TTRC), created in 1991 by the U.S. Department of Labor, delivers employment and training services. The TTRC has a large Web site that includes One-Stop/LMI, a resource devoted to training, education, and employment at the local, state, and national level. On One-Stop/LMI, you can find:

- ◆ Directories by state
- ◆ Newsletters
- ◆ Conference materials
- ◆ America's Labor Market Information System (ALMIS)

To locate ALMIS, do the following:

1. Type http://www.ttrc.doleta.gov
2. On the TTRC home page, click on One-Stop/LMI to access the information.

Additional training resources

The following are additional Web sites that offer advice on training your employees:

National Business Association (NBA)
http://www.nationalbusiness.org

Established in 1982 to support and educate entrepreneurs, small business owners, and professionals.

De Vry Institute
http://www.devry.edu

De Vry has 14 campuses in the United States and Canada that provide training in electronics technology, telecommunications management, computer information systems, business operations, technical management, and accounting.

Sandler Sales Institute
http://www.sandler.com

Offers training for your sales organization to help close more sales and make more money.

New Horizons
http://www.newhorizons.com

Offers computer training to more than 1.5 million students every year.

Information Technology Training Association (ITTA)
http://www.itta.org

A trade association for the Information Technology training industry.

New Horizons for Learning
http://www.newhorizons.org

A worldwide learning network, established in 1980, that provides newsletters, conferences, and networking opportunities.

Chapter 27

Employee Benefits

Employee benefits are expensive for the business owner. A typical benefits package that includes medical, dental, life insurance, long-term disability income, and a 401(k) plan, can cost an employer more than 10 percent of an employee's gross salary. Cost can be considerably more if workers' comp, matching Social Security, Medicare taxes, and OSHA mandates are included as part of "employee benefits."

Benefit plans are designed in a number of ways, including internal evaluations where employees are asked what they want, external surveys to see what the competition is providing, and by what is available in the market.

This chapter reviews Web sites that provide advice on employee benefits and on designing an appropriate plan to administer the benefits.

Simple IRAs; questions and answers

http://www.benefitslink.com/IRS/97-6.html

BenefitsLink
http://www.benefitslink.com

BenefitsLink has "information and services for employers sponsoring employee benefit plans, companies providing products and services for plans, and participating employees." By using the BenefitsLink search engine, you can obtain a wide variety of information on benefit plans.

For instance, if you wanted to learn more about simple IRAs, you would do the following:

1. Type http://www.benefitslink.com in your Web browser's address box and press Enter.
2. On the BenefitsLink home page, click on Search BenefitsLink.
3. After you reach the BenefitsLink Search Engine page, type "SIMPLE IRAs; Questions and Answers" (no quotes) in the What are you looking for? box and then click on [Search].
4. On the BenefitsLink Search Results page, click on IRS Notice 97-6 for a complete description.

Advanced plan design questions and answers

http://www.benefitslink.com/columns/plandesign/index.html

If you were thinking about sponsoring a tax-qualified retirement plan, then you would want to review BenefitsLink's "Advanced Plan Design Questions and Answers."

To see this page, do the following:

1. Type http://www.benefitslink.com in your Web browser's address box and press Enter.
2. On the BenefitsLink home page, click on Q&A Columns.
3. After you reach the Q&A Columns page, select the Advanced Plan Design Q&A Column for a full discussion.

BenefitsLink's message boards

http://www.benefitslink.com/benefits-bin/BenefitsLinkBBS/benefitslinkbbs.cgi

BenefitsLink also sponsors various message boards. A message board is a place where you can obtain advice from other people through an e-mail message. You post a message, or question, on the bulletin board and other people have the opportunity to reply.

To see the BenefitsLink message board on retirement plans, do the following:

1. Type http://www.benefitslink.com in your Web browser's address box and press Enter.
2. On the BenefitsLink home page, click on Message Boards.
3. Once you reach the Message Boards page, click on Retirement Plans in General.

Important tips to save time and money in filing W-2s

http://www.ssa.gov/employer_info/empwage.html

Social Security Administration
http://www.ssa.gov

The Social Security Administration has been providing economic protection for Americans during the past 60 years. Social Security benefits come from five major categories:

1. Retirement
2. Disability
3. Family benefits
4. Survivors
5. Medicare

If you are filing W-2s for your employees, then you may want some helpful advice from the SSA.

To see some tips from the IRS, do the following:

1. Type http://www.ssa.gov in your Web browser's address box and press Enter.
2. On the SSA home page, scroll down and click on Employer Wage Reporting an improved and expanded guide to Wage Reporting for Employers.
3. On the Help for Employers page, select the [Wage Reporting Tips] button.

Employer costs for employee compensation

http://stats.bls.gov/news.release/ecec.toc.htm

U.S. Department of Labor
http://stats.bls.gov/blshome.html

The U.S. Department of Labor, through its Bureau of Labor Statistics, publishes the "Employer Costs for Employee Compensation." For instance, in 1997, private industry paid an average salary of $17.97 per hour, of which $13.04 per hour was for wages and salary, or 72.5 percent, and $4.93 per hour was for benefits, or 27.5 percent. These figures are broken out in many different ways, including goods versus service producing industries and white versus blue-collar occupations.

For the entire employee compensation survey, complete the following steps:

1. Type http://stats.bls.gov/blshome.html in your Web browser's address box and press Enter.
2. On the BLS home page, click on the [Publications & Research Papers] box.
3. After you reach the Publications & Research Papers page, select [News Releases] box.
4. On the News Releases page, scroll down to the Compensation & Working Conditions heading and select Employer costs for employee compensation.

Employee benefits in small private industry establishments

http://stats.bls.gov/news.release/ebs.toc.htm

Another survey published by the Bureau of Labor Statistics that will interest you is the "Employee Benefits in Small Private Industry Establishments." In this survey you will find that many small employers (less than 100 workers) offer their employees significant benefits. For instance, 66 percent of full-time workers were covered by a health benefit plan, 88 percent had paid vacation plans, and 50 percent had paid sick leave.

To see the entire BLS survey, do the following:

1. Type http://stats.bls.gov/blshome.html in your Web browser's address box and press Enter.
2. On the BLS home page, click on the [Surveys and Programs] box.
3. Once you reach the Surveys and Programs page, select the [Compensation & Working Conditions] box to get to the Employee Benefits Survey.

Total salary increase budget survey

http://www.acaonline.org/reasearch/generic/html/acareasfra000000.html

American Compensation Association
http://www.acaonline.org

The American Compensation Association (ACA) is an association of human resource specialists who manage employee compensation and benefit programs. The ACA provides information, training, and research for the entire profession. On its Web site, you can view the "Total Salary Increase Budget Survey."

Salary surveys are important to your business because they will help you to keep your salary structure competitive and retain key employees. The ACA survey also includes "other elements of total compensation, including promotional increases, indirect compensation, and stock-based compensation plans."

To view the ACA "Total Salary Increase Budget Survey," do the following:

1. In your Web browser's address box, type http://www.acaonline.org and press Enter.
2. On the ACA home page, click on the [Research] button.
3. After you reach the Research page, click on the [Total Salary Increase Budget Survey] box.

Additional employee benefit resources

For more information on employee benefit plans, you can also try some of the following Web sites.

Employee Benefit Research Institute (EBRI)
http://www.ebri.org

Started in 1978, EBRI is a nonprofit organization that "gathers, documents, analyzes, and communicates the facts that will shape the employee benefit programs of the future."

Employee Benefits Group, Inc.
http://www.ebg.com

Provides employee benefits consulting to companies worldwide.

National Association of Stock Plan Professionals
http://www.naspp.com

Consists of more than 3,500 members who design and administrate stock plans.

Benefits Information Group Insights
http://www.biginsights.com

For a fee, you can access this online subscription service of more than 213,000 welfare and retirement plans.

Benefits Interface
http://www.benefits.org

Helps Canadian employers maximize employee benefits compensation through design, communication, and administration.

International Foundation of Employee Benefit Plans
http://www.ifebp.org

The IFEBP is an educational association of more than 30,000 individuals in the employee benefits field.

Employee Benefit Resources on the Internet
http://www.mtsu.edu/~rlhannah/employee_benefits.html

Created by a professor at Middle Tennessee State University, this Web page provides a list of links and discussion groups on employee benefits.

Internet Resources
http://www.nceo.org/resource/benefit.html

Provides links to business information available on the Internet, including links for employee benefits and human resources.

Hale and Dorr Labor and Employment Bulletin
http://www.haledorr.com/publications/labor/LaborDirectory.html

Published by the law firm of Hale and Dorr, this site contains multiple labor and employment bulletins.

Chapter 28

Financial Statements

What is the difference between the balance sheet and an income statement? The balance sheet shows you where your business is at a point in time, while the income statement shows you how it got there. For instance, if you decided to start your newsletter business today and had $100 in the bank, then your balance sheet would show that your business had $100 in assets, no liabilities, and $100 in equity. If you sold a newsletter subscription tomorrow for a profit of $5, then you would have $105 in assets, no liabilities, and $105 in equity at the end of the day.

Realistic financial statements will help you obtain financing from potential investors and will serve as a control mechanism to measure profitability. Financial management is a necessity for every successful business. You must establish policies to ensure that the business is meeting its financial goals and commitments. This chapter reviews Web sites that provide advice on preparing financial statements.

Record-keeping in small business

http://www.sbaer.uca.edu/docs/publications/pub00194.txt

Small Business Advancement National Center (SBANC)
http://www.sbaer.uca.edu

The Small Business Advancement National Center (SBANC), located on the campus of the University of Central Arkansas, offers small business counseling and an electronic resource information center. The SBANC Web site contains a series of articles for entrepreneurs and small business owners.

For instance, on this site you can locate an article titled "Record-keeping in Small Business." This article stresses that an appropriate record-keeping system can determine the survival or failure of a new business...and increase the chances of staying in business and the opportunity to earn larger profits." It also addresses:

- The need for good records.
- Requirements of a good system.

♦ Methods of accounting.
♦ The accounting cycle.
♦ How to analyze your records.

For more information on record-keeping, complete the following steps:

1. In your Web browser's address box, type http://www.sbaer.uca.edu and press Enter.
2. On the SBANC home page, scroll down and click on the [Publications] box.
3. After you reach the Small Business Publications page, select Tax / Accounting from the list.
4. Now you can select the Record-keeping in Small Business article under the Tax / Accounting heading.

Edge Online financial management

http://www.edgeonline.com/main/bizbuilders/index2.shtm

Edward Lowe Foundation
http://www.lowe.org

"Business Builders," from the Edward Lowe Foundation, are a series of training modules to help you manage and grow your business. One of the "Business Builders" that you should review is called "Financial Management." This series of articles will help you to:

♦ Prepare and analyze a balance sheet.
♦ Analyze profitability.
♦ Use financial ratios.
♦ Prepare a profit and loss statement.
♦ Prepare a cash budget.
♦ Prepare a cash flow statement.

To review the "Financial Management Business Builders," do the following:

1. In your Web browser's address box, type http://www.lowe.org and press Enter.
2. On the Edward Lowe Foundation home page, click on the [Entrepreneurial Edge Online] box.
3. After you reach the Edge Online home page, scroll down and click on interactive modules under the Business Builders heading.
4. On the Business Builders page, scroll down to the Financial Management topics and review the financial statements previously mentioned.

Preparing a cash flow forecast

http://www.sb.gov.bc.ca/smallbus/workshop/cashflow.html

Canada/British Columbia Business Service Centre
http://www.sb.gov.bc.ca/smallbus/sbhome.html

The Canadian Business Service Centre, through its Online Small Business Workshop, has a series of "techniques for developing your idea, starting a new venture, and improving your existing small business." Included in the Workshop is some sound financial advice, such as "Preparing a Cash Flow Forecast." This article explains that you should prepare a cash flow forecast to monitor when your expect cash to be coming in and going out of your business.

To learn how to prepare a cash flow forecast, do the following:

1. In your Web browser's address box, type http://www.sb.gov.bc.ca/smallbus/sbhome.html and press Enter.
2. On the Business Service Centre home page, click on <u>Online Small Business Workshop</u>.
3. After you reach the Workshop page, click on <u>Preparing a Cash Flow Forecast</u>.

Maximizing your relationship with your CPA

http://ewmdws003.ibm.net/smb/smbusapub.nsf/DetailContacts/86256613005 9C0DC8525662100669454?OpenDocument

IBM Small Business Center
http://www.idm.ibm.com/smbus/

The IBM Small Business Center can help you with its Business-Building Strategies. One suggestion is to maximize your relationship with your Certified Public Accountant (CPA), who can often provide "new and innovative ways of thinking" and "intelligent advice and guidance." To make the most of this relationship, ask your CPA for a "wider range of services that may be appropriate for your business" and to "describe in layman's terms, what he/she sees behind the numbers." To read this article, do the following:

1. In your Web browser's address box, type http://www.idm.ibm.com/smbus/ and press Enter.
2. On the IBM Small Business Center home page, click on the [Resources & News] tab.
3. Once you reach the Resources & News page, scroll down and select <u>Case Studies</u>.
4. On the IBM Case Studies page, scroll down and locate the <u>Maximizing your relationship with your CPA</u> article.

Find a CPA

http://www.cpalink.com/index.html

CPA Link
http://www.cpalink.com/index.html

CPA Link is an online directory that will help you find an accounting professional in your area. You can select an accountant by industry specialization and state. Information provided in the directory listings includes:

- State society membership
- Licensed by State Board of Accountancy/Licensing
- AICPA membership status

To locate a CPA in your area, do the following:

1. In your Web browser's address box, type http://www.cpalink.com/index.html and press Enter.
2. On the CPA Link home page, choose your Industry Focus and State from the drop down boxes, then click on Find.

State CPA societies

http://www.accountingnet.com/abou/aboufr.html

AccountingNet
http://www.accountingnet.com

AccountingNet is a resource on the Internet for accountants, accounting firms, and anyone else interested in reaching the accounting community. On its Web site, you can locate the contact information for the CPA society in your state.

To find your state CPA society, do the following:

1. In your Web browser's address box, type http://www.accountingnet.com and press Enter.
2. On the AccountingNet home page, click on Research Library from the drop-down list.
3. After you reach the Research Library page, scroll down and select State CPA Societies under the Associations and Societies heading.

ADP tax calculator

http://www.adp.com/emergingbiz/tool/index.html

Automatic Data Processing
http://www.adp.com

Through its "Recruiting & Retaining Employees" information, ADP can help you determine how much payroll tax to withhold.

To try the ADP "Tax Calculator," do the following:

1. In your Web browser's address box, type http://www.adp.com and press Enter.
2. On the ADP home page, click on [Visit Our New Emerging Business Center] box.
3. After you reach the Emerging Business Services page, select the [Business Tools] button.
4. On the Business Tools page, scroll down and click on the [Tax Calculator] box.

Additional financial statement resources

The following are some additional resources you may want to examine as your prepare financial statements for your business.

EntrepreNet
http://www.enterprise.org/enet/library/be.html

Breakeven analysis. Provides "information on one of the most essential tools an entrepreneur can have for analyzing his or her current or new business venture."

Business Finance (formerly Controller Magazine)
http://www.businessfinancemag.com

Available online, this publication has "need-to-know, practical information for the financial manager."

Geocities
http://www.geocities.com

More than 1 million individuals share their thoughts through Geocities. You can find some practical finacial advice from the "Investing, Small Business, Advertising" section under the Business & Money heading.

Net Earnings
http://www.netearnings.com

Formed "to serve the financial needs of small business via the Internet," this site can help you locate links to the big accounting firms and tax software under the Tax & Accounting heading.

How To Collect Business Debts
http://www.iinet.net.au/~heath/debtbook.html

An online book from Australia, that "tells you what debt-collection methods there are, how well they work, and how to choose which to use."

American Institute of Certified Public Accountants
http://www.aicpa.org

The AICPA, with more than 300,000 members, is the professional association of accountants in the United States.

Chapter 29

Loan Information

If you are starting a new business, most of the money you will need to get it off the ground will either come from you and your partners, or from your friends and family. Sometimes it is possible for a new business to get funding from outside investors in the form of venture capital. However this is normally limited to the high-technology industries where the potential for growth is enormous and the products are truly innovative.

Once your business is off the ground and has established a track record, then you may consider getting a loan from a bank. Banks like to lend money to businesses that can provide some type of collateral. For instance, if you needed to buy a new piece of equipment, a bank might consider lending you some money for the specific purpose of buying the equipment. In the event that your business fails, the bank could then take possession of the equipment and try to recoup some of its investment in the open market. Much like the mortgage on a home.

In addition to seeking a loan from your local neighborhood bank, there are also a host of financing companies (non-banks) that you should consider. The loans that these non-banks make are usually backed by the U.S. Small Business Administration and can be used for items such as commercial real estate, new construction, business acquisitions and expansions, renovations and tenant improvements, equipment and inventory, or working capital.

This chapter reviews many of the non-bank sites that you might consider in order to obtain a loan.

Financing your business

http://www.sbaonline.sba.gov/financing/synopses.html

U.S. Small Business Administration

http://www.sbaonline.sba.gov

The U.S. Small Business Administration (SBA) provides financing for business owners through a series of loan programs. These loans are made available to small businesses that have been unsuccessful at securing financing through "normal lending channels." The SBA loan programs include:

- Loan Guaranty
- LowDoc
- FA$TRAK
- CAPLines
- International Trade
- Export Working Capital
- Pollution Control
- Minority and Women's Prequal
- Disabled Assistance
- Veteran's Loans
- Certified Development Company (504 Loan) Program

For a complete description of these SBA loan programs, do the following:

1. In your browser's address box, type http://www.sbaonline.sba.gov and press Enter.
2. After the SBA home page appears, click on the [Financing] button.
3. On the next page, locate and click on the [Loan Programs] button.
4. After you reach the Loan Programs page, select the [Synopses of Loans] button.
5. Now you can read descriptions of the loan programs listed.

Obtaining an SBA loan: five helpful hints

http://www.themoneystore.com/small_business/resource_center/articles/articl es.html

Money Store
http://www.themoneystore.com

Through The Money Store Commercial Lending Division you can borrow up to $2.5 million for commercial real estate, new construction, business acquisitions and expansions, renovations and tenant improvements, equipment and inventory, or working capital. Prior to applying for business loans, this Web site suggests you do the following:

- Get your financial house in order.
- Realistically define your goals.
- Recognize your strengths and weaknesses.
- Start early.
- Work with an experienced small business lender.

For the five helpful hints on obtaining an SBA loan, do the following:

1. Type http://www.themoneystore.com in your Web browser's address box and press Enter.
2. On the Money Store home page, click on Small Business Loans.
3. Once you reach the Small Business Loans page, select small informative articles.
4. On the Informative articles of small business lending page, you can now select Obtaining a Small Business Loan: Five Helpful Hints.

Does my business qualify for an SBA loan?

http://www.ge.com/capital/smallbiz/sb3.htm

GE Capital Small Business Finance
http://www.ge.com/capital/smallbiz/index.htm

GE Capital Small Business Finance, licensed by the U.S. Small Business Administration, provides loans up to $2 million for small businesses. These SBA loans are asset-based and "are designed to help small businesses maximize cash flow and keep pace with growth opportunities."

Usually the first question you will ask about these loans is, "Do I qualify?" According to the SBA guidelines, your business may be eligible for these loans if it meets the following requirements:

- The business is independently owned and operated.
- It is not dominant in its field.
- It meets SBA employment and sales standards.

According to GE Capital, 98 percent of all U.S. businesses fall into this category.

To learn more about how to apply for an SBA loan, do the following:

1. Type http://www.ge.com/capital/smallbiz/index.htm in your Web browser's address box and press Enter.
2. On the GE Capital home page, click on Does My Business Qualify?

Finance 101

http://www.attcapital.com/corporate/meetus/

AT&T Capital
http://www.attcapital.com

AT&T Capital Corporation, now part of the Newcourt Credit Group, also provides SBA-backed loans. Through its Web site, you can learn about the typical uses for the loans and the eligibility requirements.

To learn more about SBA loans from AT&T, do the following:

1. Type http://www.attcapital.com in your Web browser's address box and press Enter.

2. On the AT&T Capital/Newcourt home page, click on <u>AT&T Capital Corporation Tools to Grow</u>.

3. After you reach the AT&T Capital Home page, click on the [Site Guide] box.

4. On the Website Guide page, select <u>Company and Industry News</u>.

5. You will then be able to select the <u>Finance 101</u> article, which explains the SBA program.

Loan application

http://www.sbls.inter.net/

Small Business Loan Source
http://www.sbls.inter.net

The Small Business Loan Source (SBLS) is another nationally licensed SBA non-bank lender. It was established in 1989 with an authority to make loans by a charter from the federal government. SBLS specializes in SBA lending and makes loans in all 50 states.

Eligible businesses listed on its Web site include manufacturing companies, hotels and motels, restaurants, convenience stores, dry cleaners, daycare centers, small office buildings (owner occupied), office warehouses, bed and breakfasts/hunting lodges, and horse stables.

To learn more about SBLS and to print a loan application, do the following:

1. In your Web browser's address box, type http://www.sbls.inter.net and press Enter.

2. Click on the [Download an Application] box, and then follow the onscreen instructions.

SBIR proposal preparation

http://www.sbir.dsu.edu/proposalpreparation/outline.htm

Small Business Innovative Research
http://www.sbir.dsu.edu

The Small Business Innovative Research is a "Federal program that requires Federal agencies and departments to allocate part of their R & D budgets to some small company competitions." This program is available through the following agencies: National Science Foundation (NSF); the Departments of Defense, Agriculture, Commerce, Education, Energy, Health and Human Services (National Institutes of Health), Transportation; the

National Aeronautics and Space Administration (NASA); Nuclear Regulatory Commission (NRC); and Environmental Protection Agency (EPA).

To learn more about applying for one of these research grants, do the following:

1. In your Web browser's address box, type http://www.sbir.dsu.edu and press Enter.
2. On the Project SBIR West page, click on Proposal Preparation.
3. After you reach the Proposal Preparation Information page, select SBIR Proposal Outline for a complete description.

Lenders Interactive Services

http://www.lendersinteractive.com

Lenders Interactive Services (LIS) matches lenders with business owners needing a loan. This online matching service uses type of loan, dollar amount, location, and industry as lending criteria. Loans are available for accounts receivable, buyout or acquisition, commercial real estate, construction, equipment financing, expansion, franchises, and more.

To complete and submit an application online, do the following:

1. In your Web browser's address box, type http://www.lendersinteractive.com and press Enter.
2. On the LIS home page, click on the [Search for Compatible Lenders] box and follow the onscreen directions.

Additional loan information resources

The following are more sources for obtaining a loan.

Online Banking and Financial Services Directory
http://www.orcc.com/banking.htm

An online listing of banks, credit unions, and other financial organizations in the United States.

Creative Investment Research
http://www2.ari.net/cirm/

A minority-owned firm that provides information on minority- and women-owned brokerage firms and banks.

DataMerge Inc.
http://www.datamerge.com/stories/stories.cfm

Provides financing sources and advice for entrepreneurs and business owners.

Small Business Lending in the United States
http://www.sbaonline.sba.gov/SmallBusinessLending1996

Published annually by the Office of Advocacy, this guide ranks "commercial banks' lending performance to small businesses by state."

Heller First Capital
http://www.hellerfin.com/hfcc/

A national non-bank lender that participates in the SBA loan guarantee program.

America's Business Funding Directory
http://www.businessfinance.com

Using this site, you can locate potential funding sources for business and real estate projects.

Debt Counselors of America
http://www.dca.org/home.htm

An organization that provides advice for individuals on how to get out of debt.

American Bankruptcy Institute
http://www.abiworld.org

An organization that posts articles, news, and recent laws concerning bankruptcy on its Web site.

Chapter 30

Venture Capital

After you have tapped out your parents, friends, and acquaintances for money to start your new business or to fund your expansion, then it is time to try the banks and venture capitalists. Although you may initially perceive them to have deep pockets and be willing to invest in your promising new company, you may give up and try your parents, friends, and acquaintances again!

Venture capitalists invest money in new and expanding businesses. They may be wealthy individuals, such as doctors and lawyers, partnerships, or even corporations. A new business that is fortunate enough to attract venture capital funding can expect to give up a sizable piece of equity, or ownership, in return. Banks also invest in businesses, although they are not interested in ownership. They normally lend money against the assets of a business, such as accounts receivable or inventory.

This chapter reviews Web sites that describe how to obtain venture capital.

Growth company guide to investors, deal structures, and legal strategies

http://www.once.com/gcg

Venture Capital
http://www.once.com/gcg

This complete online book by Clinton Richardson offers "practical advice for growing companies and private company investors." It has definitions of words and phrases that are used in the industry by entrepreneurs and venture capitalists.

To see the book and complete definition of venture capital, do the following:

1. Type http://www.once.com/gcg in your Web browser's address box and press Enter.

2. On the GCG home page, scroll down under the Contents heading and click on <u>Venture Capital</u>.

Initial public offering
http://www.once.com/gcg

Another phrase that you might want to look up in the online book is "Initial Public Offering (IPO)." According to the guide, "IPOs refer to the first registered offering of company securities to the general population of equity investors." To learn more about IPOs, do the following:

1. In your Web browser's address box, type http://www.once.com/gcg and press Enter.
2. On the GCG home page, scroll down under the Contents section and click on IPOs (Initial Public Offerings).

A venture capital primer for small business
http://fambiz.com/contprov.cfm?ContProvCode=SBA&ID=151

NetMarquee
http://nmq.com

NetMarquee, a specialist in business-to-business Internet marketing, provides access to its extensive library of resources through its Web site. For instance, if you wanted to learn the differences between borrowing and venture capital you could review "A Venture Capital Primer for Small Business." It states, "Banks are creditors; they expect you to repay the borrowed money. Venture capital firms are owners; they hold stock in the company, adding their invested capital to its equity base."

To view information from NetMarquee, do the following:

1. In your Web browser's address box, type http://nmq.com and press Enter.
2. On the NetMarquee home page, select Financing from the drop-down list of "Search our library of 300 family business articles" and click on [Go].
3. When you reach the results page, scroll down and click on A Venture Capital Primer for Small Business.

How to raise venture capital
http://www.vcapital.com/howto.html

Venture Capital Online
http://www.vcapital.com

Venture CapitalOnline (VCOL), a service provided by Batterson Venture Partners, is for "entrepreneurs seeking venture capital and investors seeking investments in entrepreneurial high-growth companies." According to its Web site, Batterson will consider business proposals presented in a succinct plan format.

VCOL also provides some helpful advice in its article, "How To Raise Venture Capital." The company explains that in order for your business to raise venture capital, especially in startup, it must "address a large, rapidly growing market with a unique product, which is very tough to duplicate and for which there is little or no known present competition."

To read more, do the following:

1. Type http://www.vcapital.com in your Web browser's address box and press Enter.
2. On the Venture Capital Online home page, click on Venture Scene.
3. After you reach the Venture Scene, scroll down and select How to Raise Venture Capital.

National venture capital survey

http://www.pw.com/vc

Price Waterhouse LLP
http://www.pw.com

Price Waterhouse, one of the largest accounting firms, publishes the "National Venture Capital Survey" every quarter. It is a study of venture capital investments, which includes type of business (software, hardware, biotechnology), stage of investment, amount of investment, and the co-investors. If you would like to see the types of businesses raising venture capital, do the following:

1. Type http://www.pw.com/vc in your Web browser's address box and press Enter.
2. On the National Venture Capital Survey page, click on Report for a listing of results.

Venture capital firms

http://financehub.com/vc_idx.html

FinanceHub
http://financehub.com/welcomef.html

FinanceHub, a Web site maintained by InterSoft Solutions, provides information on banks, the stock market, online commerce, law, and venture capital. In addition to articles on venture capital, this Web site has a comprehensive listing of venture capital companies, consultants, and specialized law firms.

To see the FinanceHub list of venture capital companies, do the following:

1. Type http://financehub.com/welcomef.html in your Web browser's address box and press Enter.

2. On the FinanceHub home page, click on <u>Venture Capital</u>.

3. After your reach the next page, select <u>VC Firms</u> for a complete listing.

Additional venture capital resources

For additional information on raising money through venture capital, you may want to review some of the following Web sites.

IPOnet

http://www.zanax.com/iponet

Cleared by the United States SEC to sell securities online.

Business Resource Center

http://www.morebusiness.com/financing/sbic.html

Alliance Technology Ventures

http://www.atv.com/04resources/04.resources.html

ATV is a venture capital firm that manages institutional funds for investment. Provides guidelines on how to prepare a checklist of information they will require in order to review your business opportunity.

Accel Partners

http://www.accel.com/entrepreneurs/

Includes a library of articles and speeches on its Web site that are of interest to entrepreneurs in search of financing through venture capital.

Venture One

http://www.ventureone.com/entre/

Through extensive research and information products, this Web site matches growing companies with venture capitalists.

SEC—Small Business Information

http://www.sec.gov/smbus1.htm

Regulatory agency that is responsible for administering the federal securities laws.

Red Herring

http://www.redherring.com

A monthly publication for business leaders and investors that reports on high-growth markets and emerging technologies.

Directory of Resources

Following is a directory of resources that includes not only the Web sites reviewed in the book, but also a host of others that might be useful for your business plan. This list is broken down by industry.

Banks and brokerages

Ameritrade	http://www.ameritrade.com
AT&T Capital	http://www.attcapital.com
Bank of America	http://www.bankamerica.com
Bankers Trust	http://www.bankerstrust.com
Charles Schwab Online	http://www.schwab.com
Chase	http://www.chase.com
Citibank	http://www.citibank.com
Dean Witter	http://www.deanwitter.com
Dreyfus	http://www.dreyfus.com
Fidelity Investments	http://www.fidelity.com
GE Capital Small Business Finance	http://www.ge.com/capital/smallbiz/index.htm
Heller First Capital	http://www.hellerfin.com/hfcc/
J.P. Morgan	http://www.jpmorgan.com
Lombard Institutional Brokerage	http://www.lombard.com
Merrill Lynch	http://www.ml.com
Money Store	http://www.themoneystore.com/
Morningstar Mutual Funds	http://www.morningstar.net
Mutual Funds Home Page	http://www.brill.com
Online Banking and Financial Services Directory	http://www.orcc.com/banking.htm
Paine Webber	http://www.painewebber.com
Small Business Loan Source	http://www.sbls.inter.net
Smith Barney	http://www.smithbarney.com
Wells Fargo	http://www.wellsfargo.com

Business: Accounting

AccountingNet	http://www.accountingnet.com
Arthur Andersen	http://www.benlore.com/files/ emexpert1_2.html
Automatic Data Processing	http://www.adp.com
CPA Link	http://www.cpalink.com/index.html
Deloitte & Touche LLP	http://www.dtonline.com
How To Collect Business Debts	http://www.iinet.net.au/~heath/ debtbook.html
Price Waterhouse LLP	http://www.pw.com
TaxWeb	http://www.taxweb. com

Business: Financial

Accel Partners	http://www.accel.com
Alliance Technology Ventures	http://www.atv.com/index.shtml
America's Business Funding Directory	http://www.businessfinance.com
America's Small Business Financial Center	http://www.netearnings.com
Annual Reports Library	http://www.zpub.com/sf/arl
Asia Business News Interactive	http://www.abn-online.com
Bankinfo.com	http://www.bankinfo.com
Briefing.com	http://www.briefing.com
Business Wire	http://www.businesswire.com
Canada Stockwatch	http://www.canada-stockwatch.com
CEO Express	http://www.ceoexpress.com
Creative Investment Research	http://www2.ari.net/cirm/
Cyberinvest.com	http://www.cyberinvest.com
DataMerge Inc.	http://www.datamerge.com
DBC Online	http://www.dbc.com
E*Trade	http://www.etrade.com
Euromoney/Worldlink	http://www.emwl.com
Far Eastern Economic Review	http://www.feer.com
Federal Filings High Yield	http://www.fedfil.com/highyield/ comment.htm
FinanceHub	http://financehub.com/welcomef.html
FINWeb	http://www.finweb.com/
First Chicago Capital Markets	http://www.fcnbd.com/cor/fccm/ research/HTML/index.htm
First Union	http://www.firstunion.com
FreeEdgar	http://www.FreeEdgar.com

Growth Company Guide to Investors, Deal Structures, and Legal Strategies	http://www.once.com/gcg/
Holt Stock Report	http://207.67.198.21/holt/index.html
Internect Financial Database	http://www.inect.co.uk/int0024.html
Investools	http://www.investools.com
Investor's Edge	http://www.irnet.com
Investor.Net	http://www.investor.net
Investorama	http://www.investorama.com
InvestorGuide	http://www.investorguide.com
IPO Central	http://www.ipocentral.com
IPOnet	http://www.zanax.com/iponet
Kiplinger Online	http://kiplinger.com
Lenders Interactive Services	http://www.lendersinteractive.com
Money Network	http://www.finforum.com
Money Page	http://www.moneypage.com
MoneyWorld	http://www.moneyworld.co.uk
Moody's Investors Service	http://www.moodys.com
Motley Fool	http://www.fool.com
Municipal Resource Center	http://www.municipal.com
National Mortgage Rates— Date and time Stamped	http://www.microsurf.com/
NetMarquee	http://nmq.com/
NETworth	http://www.galt.com
Platt's	http://www.platts.com
Private Equity Links	http://www.envista.com/private equitylinks/index.html
Quote.com	http://www.quote.com
Reuters Moneynet	http://www.moneynet.com
Silicon Investor	http://www.techstocks.com
Standard & Poor's	http://www.stockinfo.standardpoor.com
Stock quotes from Security APL	http://www.secapl.com/cgi-bin/qs
Stockmaster	http://www.stockmaster.com
StockScreener	http://www.stockscreener.com
Street.com	http://www.thestreet.com
Streeteye	http://www.streeteye.com
TechInvestor	http://www.techweb.com/investor
Thomson Investors Network	http://www.thomsoninvest.net
Venture Capital Finance Master Resources Page	http://www.autonomy.com/venture.htm
Venture Capital Online	http://www.vcapital.com/
Venture One	http://www.ventureone.com/entre/
Wall Street City	http://www.wallstreetcity.com

Wall Street Directory Inc.	http://www.wsdinc.com
Wall Street Research Net	http://www.wsrn.com
Web Street Securities	http://www.webstreetsecurities.com
Wright Investors' Service	http://www.wisi.com

Business: General

555-1212.com	http://www.555-1212.com
Access Franchise Directory Online	http://www.entremkt.com/access/
Advanced Benefits Services Inc.	http://net-gate.com/~abs/abs.html
American Express	http://www.americanexpress. com/smallbusiness
AT&T Toll-Free Internet Directory	http://att.net/dir800
Benefits Information Group Insights	http://www.biginsights.com
BenefitsLink	http://www.benefitslink.com
BenefitsLink's Message Boards	http://www.benefitslink.com/ discussion.shtml
Big Bertha	http://www.ok2golf.com/gbb_main.htm
Big Yellow	http://www.bigyellow.com
BigBook	http://www.bigbook.com
BIZ*INFO*SEARCH	http://www.bizinfosearch.com/
bplans.com!	http://www.bplans.com/index1.html
Bregstein's Business Resource Center	http://www.chesco.com/~rbreg
Bridge News	http://www.bridge.com/serv/ PVtoplvl.htm
Business Incorporating Guide	http://www.corporate.com/home.htm
Business Resource Center	http://www.morebusiness.com
Business Savvy	http://www.businesssavvy.com/ nfhome.html
Center for Family Business	http://nmq.com/necfb
ComFind	http://www.comfind.com
Commercial Real Estate Eastern United States Guide	http://www.com-re.com/
Companies Online	http://www.companiesonline.com
Convenience.Net	http://www.c-store.com/
CorpAmerica	http://www.corpamerica.com/ incorporate.html
Cyberpreneur's Guide to the Internet	http://asa.ugl.lib.umich.edu/ chdocs/cyberpreneur/Cyber.html
De Vry Institute	http://www.devry.edu/
Dismal Scientist	http://www.dismal.com
Dow Jones Business Directory	http://businessdirectory.dowjones.com
Dun & Bradstreet, Inc.	http://www.dnb.com/

e-land	http://www.e-land.com/e-lists_pages/ best_business_e-lists.shtml
Employee Benefits Group, Inc.	http://www.ebg.com
Franchise Handbook: On-Line	http://www.franchise1.com
FranInfo	http://www.franinfo.com/
Fuld & Company, Inc.	http://www.fuld.com
Hispanic Business	http://www.hispanstar.com
Hoover's Online	http://www.hoovers.com
IBM	http://ns.idm.ibm.com/
IBM Small Business Center	http://www.idm.ibm.com/smbus/
Ideas Exchange	http://www.rimart.com
Income Opportunities Online	http://www.incomeops.com/
Industry Research Desk	http://www.virtualpet.com/ industry/rdindex2.htm
Industry.Net	http://www.industry.net
Infotrade Online Services Tower	http://www.infotradeonline. co.uk/index.htm
Institute of Management and Administration	http://www.ioma.com/index.html
Investext Group	http://investext.com/
Intuit Small Business	http://www.quicken.com/small_business.
JapanBizTech	http://www.japanbiztech.com
Kurtus Technologies	http://www.ronkurtus.com/ kurtech/default.htm
Lore International Institute	http://www.lorenet.com/
MoneyHunter	http://www.moneyhunter.com/
Mr. Coffee	http://www.mrcoffeeconcepts.com/ office/mcc120.htm
Net Earnings	http://www.netearnings.com
New Horizons	http://www.newhorizons.com/
Nexxus	http://www.nexxushair.com
Palo Alto Software Inc.	http://www.pasware.com
Poland Spring	http://auburn.maine.com/ tse/poland-me/psbco/welcome.html
Real Estate Information Network	http://www.reinet.com/
Real Estate Resources in the Southeast	http://www.realty-resources.com/
Researchmag.com	http://www.researchmag.com
ResourceNet	http://www.c-store.com
Sandler Sales Institute	http://www.sandler.com
SiteNet	http://www.sitenet.com
Smart Business Supersite	http://www.smartbiz.com
Switchboard	http://www.switchboard.com

Thomas Register of Manufacturers   http://www.thomasregister.com:8000
Web 100   http://www.w100.com
WestWard Pay Strategies   http://www.westwardpay.com
WhoWhere   http://www.whowhere.com
www.REALTOR.com   http://www.realtors.com/
Yahoo Small Business   http://smallbusiness.yahoo.com.

Business: Legal

Advertising Law Internet Site   http://www.webcom.com/
~lewrose/home.html

Chemical Patents Plus   http://casweb.cas.org/chempatplus/
Hale and Dorr Labor and Employment
Bulletin   http://www.haledorr.com/publications/
labor/LaborDirectory.html

IBM   http://patent.womplex.ibm.com
InterNet Bankruptcy Library   http://bankrupt.com
MicroPatent   http://www.micropat.com
Nolo Press Self Help Law Center   http://www.nolo.com/about.html
Practicing Attorney's Home Page   http://www.legalethics.com/pa/
main.html

Securities Fraud and Investor   http://www.securitieslaw.com
Protection
Thomson & Thomson   http://www.thomson-thomson.com
West's Legal Directory   http://www.wld.com
WWW Virtual Law Library   http://www.law.indiana.edu

Business: Marketing

$elling.com   http://www.selling.com
Ad/Vantage Pawluk   http://www.pawluk.com/pages/
pawluk.htm

American Demographics /   http://www.demographics.com/
Marketing Tools   index.html
American List Counsel   http://www.amlist.com
Business Research Lab   http://www.busreslab.com
Database America   http://www.databaseamerica.com/
html/index.htm

Direct Marketing Plaza   http://www.dmplaza.com
Gallup Organization   http://www.gallup.com
Guerilla Marketing Online   http://www.gmarketing.com
Hamilton & Bond Advertising   http://www.marketus.net/index.html
Idea Site for Business   http://www.ideasiteforbusiness.com
iMarket, Inc.   http://www.imarketinc.com

Inmark Services Inc.	http://www.inmrk.com
Lodestone Research	http://www.lodestone. com
Market Research Center	http://www.asiresearch.com
Market Research Roudtable	http://www.drgutah.com/mrrc/ mrrc.html
Marketing World by Marketing Masters	http://www.mmasters.com
PR Newswire	http://www.prnewswire.com
Survey Sampling, Inc.	http://www.ssisamples.com/
Wilson Internet Services	http://www.wilsonweb.com/

Business: SOHO

Advanced Business Consulting	http://addcom.clever.net/abc/
AT&T Small Business Information	http://www.att.com/small_business
Bathrobe 'til 10	http://www.slip.net/~sfwave
Biz Op, the Home Business Opportunity Center	http://www.bizopp.com/
BizProWeb	http://www.bizproweb.com
BizResource	http://www.bizresource.com
Business Resource Center	http://www.morebusiness.com
Business@Home	http://www.gohome.com
CyberPreneur	http://www.cyberpreneur.com
Entrepreneur Resource Center	http://www.be-your-own-boss.com
Entrepreneur's Help Page	http://www.tannedfeet.com
Entrepreneur's Mind	http://www.benlore.com
Entrepreneurs on the Web	http://www.eotw.com
Excite Small Business	http://quicken.excite.com/ small_business/
Geocities	http://www.geocities.com
Home Business Institute	http://www.hbiweb.com
How To Run A Successful Computer Training Business	http://www.bizcafe.com/ceshowto.html
How-To Marketing Library	http://mindlink.net/mej/howto.htm
Idea Café	http://www.ideacafe.com
Let's Talk Business Network	http://www.ltbn.com
Lycos Small Business	http://www.lycos.com/resources/ smallbiz/
Microsoft Small Business Resource	http://www.microsoft.com/smallbiz/
Opportunities for Women in Small Business	http://www.mindspring.com/ ~higley/project.htm
Small and Home Based Business Links	http://www.bizoffice.com

Small Business Advisor	http://www.isquare.com
Small Business Publications	http://www.pueblo.gsa.gov/smbuss.htm
Small Business Resource Center	http://www.webcom.com/seaquest/sbrc/ welcome.html
SoHo Central	http://www.hoaa.com/
SOHO Guidebook	http://www.toolkit.cch.com/
Visa Small Business Site	http://www.visa.com/cgi-bin/vee/ fb/smbiz/main.html?2+0
Visa's SmallBiz Insider	http://www.entrepreneurmag.com/visa/
Working Solo	http://www.workingsolo.com
Yahoo Small Business Information	http://www.yahoo.com/Business_and _Economy/Small_Business_Information/
Your Company: The Site for	http://pathfinder.com/money/yourco/ Small Business

Education

Accounting Web	http://www.rutgers.edu/Accounting/
Business Resources on the Web: Small Business	http://www.idbsu.edu/carol/smallbus.htm
Center for the Study of Work Teams	http://www.workteams.unt.edu
DaVinci's Inventor Homepage!	http://sulcus.berkeley.edu/Invention
EGOPHER: The Saint Louis University Entrepreneurship Gopher	http://www.slu.edu/eweb/egopher.html
Employee Benefit Resources on the Internet	http://www.mtsu.edu/~rlhannah/ employee_benefits.html
Employee Relations Discussion Lists	http://www.mtsu.edu/~rlhannah/ erlists.html
eWeb	http://www.slu.edu/eweb/
Fairmodel	http://fairmodel.econ.yale.edu
International Business Resources	http://ciber.bus.msu.edu/busres.htm
MIT Entrepreneurs Club	http://www.mit.edu:8001/activities/ e-club/e-club-home.html
National SBDC Research Network	http://www.smallbiz.suny.edu
Network for Excellence in Manufacturing Online	http://www.nemonline.org/
Princeton University Survey Research Center	http://www.princeton.edu/~abelson/ index.html
Securities Class Action Clearinghouse	http://securities.stanford.edu
Small Business Advancement National Center	http://www.sbaer.uca.edu
Small Business Innovative Research	http://www.sbir.dsu.edu

University of Washington	http://weber.u.washington.edu/~dev/
Villanova Center for Information Law and Policy	http://www.law.vill.edu
workindex.com	http://www.workindex.com/workindex/

Government

BidCast!	http://www.bidcast.com
Bureau of Economic Analysis	http://www.bea.doc.gov
Bureau of Labor Statistics	http://stats.bls.gov/ebshome.htm
Business Resource Center	http://www.morebusiness.com
Canada Business Service Centre	http://www.cbsc.org
Canada/British Columbia Business Service Centre	http://www.sb.gov.bc.ca/smallbus/ sbhome.html
Committee on Small Business	http://www.senate.gov/~sbc/
Edgar	http://www.sec.gov/edgarhp.htm
Federal Deposit Insurance Corporation	http://www.fdic.gov
Federal Marketplace	http://www.fedmarket.com
Federal Trade Commission	http://www.ftc.gov
Fedmart	http://www.fedmart.com
Foundation for Enterprise	http://www.fed.org/
GovCon	http://www.govcon.com
Guide to the Small Business Administration	http://www.geocities.com/WallStreet/2172
House Small Business Committee	http://www.house.gov/smbiz/
Immigration Central	http://www.wave.net/upg/immigration/
Internal Revenue Service	http://www.irs.ustreas.gov/prod/ cover.html
International Trade Administration	http://www.ita.doc.gov
Missouri Business Assistance Center	http://www.ecodev.state.mo.us/mbac/ default.htm
Office of Small and Disadvantaged Business Utilization	http://osdbuweb.dot.gov
SBA Office of Women's Business Ownership	http://www.sbaonline.sba.gov/ womeninbusiness/
SEC—Small Business Information	http://www.sec.gov/smbus1.htm
Service Corps of Retired Executives	http://www.scn.org/civic/score-online
Small Business Development Centers	http://www.businessfinance.com/ sbdc.htm
Small Business Innovative Research	http://www.sbir.dsu.edu
Small Business Lending in the United States	http://www.sbaonline.sba.gov/ SmallBusinessLending1996

Small Business Opportunities — http://www.ustreas.gov/treasury/services/services.html

Social Security Administration — http://www.ssa.gov

STAT-USA — http://www.stat-usa.gov

THOMAS — http://thomas.loc.gov

Training Technology Resource Center — http://www.ttrc.doleta.gov

U.S. Bureau of Labor Statistics — http://www.bls.gov

U.S. Business Advisor — http://www.business.gov

U.S. Census Bureau — http://www.census.gov

U.S. Copyright Office — http://www.lcweb.loc.gov/copyright/

U.S. Department of Housing and Urban Development — http://www.hud.gov/core.html

U.S. Department of Labor — http://stats.bls.gov/blshome.html

U.S. Geological Survey — http://www.usgs.gov/

U.S. Patent and Trademark Office — http://www.uspto.gov

U.S. Small Business Administration — http://www.sbaonline.sba.gov

White House Conference on Small Business — http://www.whcsb.com

Magazines

Advertising Age — http://www.adage.com

Business Finance — http://www.businessfinancemag.com

Business Start-Ups Online — http://www.entrepreneurmag.com

Business Week Magazine — http://www.businessweek.com

Controller Magazine — http://www.controllermag.com

Entrepreneur Magazine — http://www.entrepreneurmag.com

Forbes Magazine — http://www.forbes.com

Fortune Magazine — http://pathfinder.com/fortune/

Franchise UPDATE Publications — http://www.franchise-update.com

Harvard Business Review — http://www.hbsp.harvard.edu/frames/groups/hbr/index.html

Home Office Computing/Small Business Computing — http://www.smalloffice.com

HR Magazine — http://www.shrm.org/hrmagazine

Ideas Digest Online Center for Innovation — http://www.ideas.wis.net

Inc. Magazine — http://www.inc.com

Macfadden Business Communications Group — http://www.csnews.com

Money Daily — http://pathfinder.com/money/moneydaily/latest

Money Magazine	http://moneymag.com
National Directory of Magazines	http://www.mediafinder.com/ mag_home.cfm
Red Herring	http://www.redherring.com
Sales & Marketing Management	http://www.salesandmarketing.com
SalesDoctors Magazine	http://salesdoctors.com
Selling Power Magazine	http://www.sellingpower.com
Success Magazine	http://www.successmagazine.com
Upside	http://www.upside.com
Workforce Magazine	http://www.workforceonline.com
Worth Online	http://www.worth.com

Newspapers

AFX-Asia	http://www.indoexchange.com/afx
American City Business Journals	http://www.amcity.com
The Atlanta Journal-Constitution	http://www.accessatlanta.com/ajc/
Barron's Online	http://www.barrons.com
Boston Globe	http://www.globe.com
Chicago Sun-Times	http://www.suntimes.com/index/
Chicago Tribune	http://www.chicago.tribune.com
Crain's New York Business	http://www.crainsny.com
Electronic Recruiting News	http://www.interbiznet.com/hrstart.html
Financial Times	http://www.ft.com
Houston Chronicle	http://www.chron.com
International Herald Tribune	http://www.franchiseintl.com
Investor's Business Daily	http://www.investors.com
London Times	http://www.the-times.co.uk
Los Angeles Times	http://www.latimes.com
The Miami Herald	http://www.herald.com
National Directory of Newsletters	http://www.mediafinder.com/ newsletters/nlr1970.cfm
The New York Times	http://www.nytimes.com
Newspage	http://www.newspage.com
Newspapers Online	http://www.newspapers.com
Philadelphia Online: Inquirer and Daily News	http://www.phillynews.com
San Francisco Chronicle	http://www.sfgate.com/chronicle/
San Jose Mercury News	http://www2.sjmercury.com
Singapore Business Times Online	http://biztimes.asia1.com
St. Louis Post-Dispatch	http://www.stlnet.com
USA Today	http://www.usatoday.com
The Wall Street Journal	http://interactive.wsj.com

Washington Times National
Weekly Edition

http://www.washtimes-weekly.com

Organizations and associations

ADA InfoNet	http://www.ada-infonet.org
AFL-CIO	http://www.aflcio.org/home.htm
American Arbitration Association	http://www.adr.org
American Association of Advertising Agencies	http://www.commercepark.com/AAAA
American Association of Individual Investors	http://www.aaii.org
American Bankruptcy Institute	http://www.abiworld.org
American Bar Association	http://www.abanet.org
American Compensation Association	http://www.acaonline.org
American Institute of Certified Public Accountants	http://www.aicpa.org
American Marketing Association	http://www.ama.org/
American Renaissance Society	http://inren.net/amren/amren.html
American Society for Training and Development	http://www.astd.org/index.html
American Society of Association Executives	http://www.asaenet.org
Association of Direct Marketing Agencies	http://www.cyberdirect.com/ADMA
Association of Mass Merchandiser Vendors	http://www.ammv.com
Association of Small Business Development Centers	http://www.nafta.net/samples/asbdcdir.txt
Benefits Interface	http://www.benefits.org
Better Business Contacts	http://maui.netwave.net/bbc
C-Store Central	http://www.cstorecentral.com
Capital Venture	http://www.capitalventure.com
Colloquy—The Quarterly Frequency Marketing Newsletter	http://www.colloquy.org
Council of American Survey Research Organizations	http://www.casro.org
Debt Counselors of America	http://www.dca.org/home.htm
Direct Marketing Association	http://www.the-dma.org
Disability Forum	http://www.eease.com/disability/
Edward Lowe Foundation	http://www.lowe.org/mission.htm
Employee Benefit Research Institute	http://www.ebri.org
Employee Relations Web Picks!	http://www.nyper.com

Employers Group	http://www.hronline.org/index.html
EntrepreNet	http://www.enterprise.org/enet/
EntreWorld	http://www.entreworld.org
Family Business Roundtable	http://www.fbrinc.com
Find/SVP	http://www.findsvp.com
Home Office Association of America	http://www.hoaa.com
Information Technology Training Association	http://www.itta.org
International Development Research Council	http://www.sitenet.com/idrcnet/
International Foundation of Employee Benefit Plans	http://www.ifebp.org
International Franchise Association	http://www.franchise.org/resources/ links.html
International Society for Performance Improvement	http://www.ispi.org
Internet Public Library	http://www.ipl.org
Internet Resources	http://www.nceo.org/resource/ resource.html
Investor Protection Trust	http://www.investorprotection.org
National Association for Female Executives	http://www.nafe.com
National Association for the Self-Employed	http://www.membership.com/NASE
National Association of Industrial and Office Parks	http://www.naiop.org
National Association of Securities Dealers	http://www.nasdr.com/2700.htm
National Association of Stock Plan Professionals	http://www.naspp.com
National Business Association	http://www.nationalbusiness.org
National Federation of Independent Business	http://www.nfibonline.com
New Horizons for Learning Professional Associations and Institutes	http://www.newhorizons.org http://www.geocities.com/Wall Street/4332/associat.htm
Research Institute for Small & Emerging Business	http://www.riseb.org
Sales and Marketing Executives International	http://www.smei.org
Society for Human Resource Management	http://www.shrm.org
Society of Competitive Intelligence Professionals	http://www.scip.org

SOHO America   http://work.soho.org
WomenBiz   http://www.frsa.com/womenbiz
WorldOpinion   http://www.worldopinion.com/home.qry

Stock exchanges

American Stock Exchange   http://www.amex.com
Chicago Board of Trade   http://www.cbot.com
Chicago Board Options Exchange http://www.cboe.com
Chicago Mercantile Exchange   http://www.cme.com
Fund Alarm   http://www.fundalarm.com
Italian Stock Exchange   http://www.borsaitalia.it
Kansas City Board of Trade   http://www.kcbt.com
London Stock Exchange   http://www.londonstockex.co.uk
Montreal Exchange   http://www.me.org
Nasdaq   http://www.nasdaq.com
Nasdaq Newsroom   http://www.nasdaqnews.com
New York Cotton Exchange   http://www.nyce.com
New York Mercantile Exchange   http://www.nymex.com
New York Stock Exchange   http://www.nyse.com
Oslo Stock Exchange   http://nettvik.no/finansen/kurser
Paris Bourse   http://www.bourse-de-paris.fr
Philadelphia Stock Exchange   http://www.phlx.com
Tel Aviv Stock Exchange   http://www.tase.co.il
Tokyo Stock Exchange   http://www.tse.or.jp/eindex.html

Television

Bloomberg Personal   http://www.bloomberg.com
CNN   http://www.cnnfn.com
Court TV Small Business   http://www.courttv.com
    Law Center
EBN Interactive   http://www.ebn.co.uk
Financial Times Television   http://www.ftvision.com

Index

About
the Author

The author, Robert T. Gorman, has more than 10 years of experience in business planning functions in the telecommunications industry. His positions have included developing business plans, creating marketing proposals, analyzing competitive pricing strategies, conducting market research, preparing financial reports, and managing a set of products. He also started a computer software company specializing in sales and marketing applications.